Dynamics of
Corporate America
& Innovation

Dynamics of Corporate America & Innovation

First Edition

Matthias I. Chijioke

DYNAMICS OF CORPORATE AMERICA & INNOVATION
FIRST EDITION

iUniverse books may be ordered through booksellers or by contacting:

iUniverse
1663 Liberty Drive
Bloomington, IN 47403
www.iuniverse.com
1-800-Authors (1-800-288-4677)

Because of the dynamic nature of the Internet, any web addresses or links contained in this book may have changed since publication and may no longer be valid. The views expressed in this work are solely those of the author and do not necessarily reflect the views of the publisher.

Thus, both the author and publisher hereby disclaim any liabilities for all unintended use of the book.

The goal of this book is to educate and provide professional information regarding the contents covered. The author took reasonable care to ensure that the contents and facts presented are accurate as of the date of publication. Therefore, neither the author nor the publisher assumes any responsibility for any errors or omissions. Thus, both the author and publisher disclaim any liabilities for all unintended use of the book.

Any people depicted in stock imagery provided by Thinkstock are models, and such images are being used for illustrative purposes only.
Certain stock imagery © Thinkstock.

For Global Distribution

ISBN: 978-1-5320-0684-5 (sc)
ISBN: 978-1-5320-0685-2 (e)

Library of Congress Control Number: 2016916125

Print information available on the last page.

iUniverse rev. date: 12/30/2016

To all contemporary American business students and the global posterity of business professionals.

Contents

Exhibits and Tables

List of Figures

Preface

The Dynamics of Corporate America and Innovation reflect my many years of academic research work. The thought of writing a book that would contribute to understanding the core principles of business administration, strategic management, innovation management, global supply chain management, information systems management, e-commerce, and business models was invigorating. This book's seven chapters are easy to read, and it includes a separate index, appendix, and glossary to enhance the reader's business intuition.

Chapter 1 introduces the dynamics of corporate America and addresses the nature of business structure and much more. In chapter 2, I present elements of business ownership in corporate America. Chapter 3 introduces the nature of innovation. Chapter 4 introduces the global supply chain, and chapter 5 introduces elements of information systems. Chapter 6 presents business and strategic management techniques in corporate America; while chapter 7 summarizes the book's major points. The glossary explains some of the business jargon used in the book. My attempt was to make it straightforward and easy to understand. The index identifies key words and names mentioned in the book.

Acknowledgments

The publication of this book would not have come to fruition without inspiration and support from the Almighty God, so I acknowledge my indebtedness to Him first. I also acknowledge my dear wife of twenty-nine years of marriage, Ola Chikerenma Chijioke, and my four beautiful children: Uzondu, Chibueze, Obinna, and Nnaemeka for their countless support and contributions to making the publication of this book a success. I would also like to thank the following members of the College of Management and Technology, Walden University: Freda Turner, Ph.D. Program Director; Irene Williams, Ph.D. Chairperson, Doctoral Study Committee; and Kevin Davies, Ph.D. Doctoral Committee Member. These faculty members were highly instrumental academically in my aspiration to write this book. I am also greatly indebted to a host of other contributors and the scholarly sources of this book—the seminal works, the peer-reviewed articles, and other sources referenced.

Chapter 1

Introduction

The dynamics of corporate America are unique and phenomenal. This process continues to stand the test of time because of its structural background. A good economic system is one that combines the freedom of individual buyers and sellers and the role of government. Of the three primary economic systems—capitalism, socialism, and the mixed economy—it is only the mixed economy that allows the interaction of sellers and buyers with the combined functions of government. In the mixed economy of a capitalistic open-market society, households own natural resources of labor and capital and then exchange these resources in the market for income. Businesses pay wages, rent, and interest; and government levies taxes on both individuals and businesses. This basic circular flow requires both consumers and government spending for the exchange of goods and services within the society. Much more, strategy plays predominant role to sustain any economic systems and business organizations.

Thus, organizational leaders need to develop an increase and proactive understanding of strategies to sustain business operations. Businesses need an awareness of the significance of the concept of profitability to an enterprise. The goal of this book is to ascertain strategies to sustain business operations. To achieve this objective, I apply the Bertalanffy's general systems theory (GST) and stakeholder theory (ST) as the two conceptual frameworks in the research. One of the major findings of this study includes developing strategies and policies (a) facilitating the creation of new markets, (b) encouraging opportunities for sustainable growth, (c) developing policies for securing human and physical capital, and (d) gaining competitive advantages through employee participation.

Strategies to Sustain Business Operations

The word strategy is a Greek word originated by the military. Current business strategy emerged as a field of learning and practice in the 1960s; before that time, the terms strategy and competition rarely appeared in popular literature. According to Mintzberg (1987), there are five elements of strategy: (1) plan, (2) pattern, (3) position, (4) ploy, and (5) perspective. Alluding to that approach was identical to a directed cause of action to achieve set goals with a certain degree of consistency, identifying products or brands intended to undermine or maneuver competitors. Thus, strategy is more than long-term planning; it is a cause of action to achieve a set objective with precision and persistence to undermine competition. Every business, whether large or small, needs rebounding financial results as an indicator of the firm's effectiveness. It is one thing to make profits, and another thing to ensure sustainable growth. There are many different strategies to maintain business operations. These strategies include the following:

(a) utilizing the concepts of market orientation and entrepreneurial policies to create new markets,
(b) establishing new funding sources through venture capital and equity funding,
(c) increasing profitable ventures and investing in new technology,
(d) becoming a result-oriented firm through the reduction of waste and abuse, and
(e) gaining competitive advantage by encouraging employees' participation in decision-making.

The American economy is one of the few open mixed economies in the world, allowing corporate American business ownerships alongside government business ownership. The contributions of corporate America continue to demonstrate that countries or societies thrive when they allow full participation of both the private and the public sectors in their economy. The US economy continues to be one of the most thriving economies in the world. It consists of both private and public sectors. The sectors are mutually exclusive, as depicted in figure 2.1, the circular flow model (private and public sectors). The sectors complement each other in the dynamics of the American economy.

Let us consider the US Post Office as an example of a public sector business. As has been seen, with the emergence of a world increasingly dependent on e-mails and social media, the US Post Office has recently struggled financially and has applied various cost-saving strategies to remain relevant, including reducing daily work hours from eight hours to five hours for its employees. The US Post Office had over $100 billion in debt and unfunded liabilities; whereas FedEx, a private sector company, made a profit of over $8 billion in the last five years.[1] As you can see, the private sector becomes the catalyst driving American economic power.

The United States has one of the largest numbers of small-medium enterprises (SMEs). According to the Executive Office of the President of the United States (2014), there are 30 million small-medium enterprises.[2] Furthermore, 16 percent of the world's millionaires inherited their fortune, whereas 47 percent of millionaires are business owners, and 23 percent of world millionaires are paid skilled workers.[3] When one hears the term *corporate America*, what comes to mind? Perhaps, the answers that come to mind include the amalgamation of conglomerates, or the multinational corporations. Yes, the individual may be right; however, corporate America is much more than that. Corporate America is not only an organizational name, like Corporate America, a corporation headquartered in Boston, Massachusetts. Corporate America in this book is also a concept and an embodiment of all the above and much more. Of course, one cannot define corporate America in a simple sentence. This book on corporate America and innovation is an embodiment of concepts that have not only engineered and unified the United States of America as a country but transformed trade and industry and gave new meaning to our current existence globally.

Historically, the American economy offers high wages, more than those of other major economies, attracting immigrants by the millions. An overview of corporations in the United States with narratives of how they started is illuminating and enlightening and worth the effort and time of further exploration. The American colonies moved from marginally successful colonial economies to a small, farming economy, and thus became independent of England in 1776. Furthermore, they also freed themselves from the tyranny of the English and control by corporations that not only subdued wealth but also dominated free trade. After political independence, the quest for economic freedom began to emerge. By the creation of legislation, corporations became artificial persons with rights and liabilities.

Corporations can own properties, sue creditors, and become plaintiffs in lawsuits. Corporate charters from different states were instrumental in limiting the boundaries of corporate powers until now. State legislation regulated corporations in America, imposing restrictions or allowing them by any means to influence public policy, elections, and other realms of American society.

Public corporations sell their shares on the stock market. The United States has one of the world's largest and most influential financial markets.[4] The New York Stock Exchange is by far the biggest global capital market. The current estimate is that American investment in foreign countries totaled $3.3 trillion, whereas foreign investment in the United States totaled $2.4 trillion.[5] Corporate America is the hub upon which the wheels of corporate fortune thrive in the United States. Of course, the American economy continues to be one of the most thriving economies in the world. The business sector plays a significant role in every major economic system. The determination of business ownership and the production and distribution of goods and services within a society require not only economic decisions but also innovation management. Over the years, these choices have contributed to America's economic greatness. Thus, it is easy to see the significance of some questions such as (a) what is a business model? (b) What is innovation? What role does technology play in business? Without a doubt, failure to recognize innovation and its dual role in business management is a recipe for business failure.

There are different types of innovation. Innovation is the result of an interactive process of knowledge mining, application, and diffusion.[6] Innovation is a pivot upon which the wheels of business management thrive. Innovation also promotes creativity in an organization. If a business stops innovating, it stops being relevant. The significance of knowledge interactions for innovation continues to challenge today's managers and other organizational leaders. Business does not exist in a vacuum; therefore, corporate social responsibility is an operating corporate overhead cost in the portfolio of most organizational leaders. There are various business models. One thing is that a good business model should contain both entrance and exit strategies. Most business models lacking these two key factors—both entrance and exit strategies—fail and become dysfunctional. Many small and large businesses with dynamic business models become extinct after three to five years of operation.

Innovation is the bedrock of transformational knowledge in human history. Information technology sets the pace to maximize profits in an organization. Therefore, innovation management is the decision made to accomplish sustainable enterprises and economic reality that connects industry, society, and the environment. In corporate America, technology plays a predominant role in leading the global marketplace. Firms and individual countries have gained tremendously from the competitive advantage. Countries may become technological leaders in developing or advancing a particular technology and marketing its acquired technical advantage via licensing.

The supply chain is the business concept used to form alliance or partnership relationships laterally or horizontally between one business and another to profit. Global supply chain management (SCM) is a process of managing the supply-chain globally and/or nationally in order to gain competitive advantage. Supply chain management is one of the fastest and the most proficient method of running a business.[7] The primary goal and objective of SCM is to increase competitive advantages, adding value and reducing costs globally. Specialization, competency, and the concept of the global supply chain emerged in corporate America in the 1980s to 1990s. This period witnessed in its wake the neglect of vertical integration and outsourcing of those functions to partners. The specialization model resulted in manufacturing and distribution networks composed of various individual supply chains specific to suppliers, producers, and consumers that came together to manufacture, design, distribute, market, sell, and service products.

Competition in the marketplace defines an organizational strategy. Porter's Five Forces, as depicted in figure 5.2, evaluate the competitive intensity of the organization's industry by analyzing the market in five dimensions. Thus, organizational structure is the driving force behind operations and the foundation upon which both short-term and long-term decisions come to fruition. Strategic business management is the critical function in management that coordinates the efforts of people to accomplish goals and objectives by using available resources to minimize cost and increase output, productivity, and profitability. Business management also involves organizational leaders setting attainable goals for the accomplishment of various objectives within an organization. The perception is that an organization is a living organism that needs to be in a consistent state of equilibrium. Hence, a system contains all the components that make up the collection of its parts and the information that the organization needs to remain relevant.

Figure 1.1
Corporate America: Resource combinations and rewards.

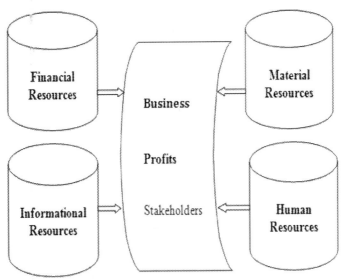

Source: *Foundation of Business - (Price, Hughes, & Kapoor, 2011)*

Chapter 2

The Dynamics of Corporate America

If you're walking down the right path and you're willing to keep walking, eventually you'll make progress.
—Barack Obama

I always did something that I was a little not ready to do. I think that is how you grow. When there's a moment of Wow, I'm not so sure that I can do this, and you push through those moments, it's then that you have a breakthrough. Sometimes that's a sign that something really great is about to happen. You're about to grow and learn a lot more about yourself.
—Denise Morrison, CEO of Campbell Soup

Corporate America is the hub upon which the wheels of corporate fortune thrive in the United States. Table 1 discloses the top ten largest corporations in terms of revenue and employment in 2014. These ten largest corporations are Wal-Mart Stores, Inc., with a total employee count of 2.2 million worldwide and total revenues of $476,294 million; ExxonMobil, with a total employee count of 76,900 and worldwide revenues of $411,939 million; Chevron, with a total employee count of 64,700 and worldwide revenues of $211,970 million; Berkshire Hathaway, with a total employee count of 316,000 and total worldwide revenues of $194,673 million; Apple, with a total employee count of 80,300 and worldwide revenues of $182,795 million; General Motors, with a total employee count of 284,000 and global revenues of $155,929 million; General Electric, with a total employees of 307,000 and a worldwide revenues of $148,589 million; Ford Motor Company, with a total employee count of 164,000 and worldwide revenues of $144,007 million; Valero Energy, with a total employee count of 10,000 and worldwide revenues of $130,844 million; and Phillips 66, with a total employee count of 13,500 and worldwide revenues of $130,180 million. These are the current powerhouses controlling almost all the corporate spectrum in the multinational oil industry, multinational retail industry, and technology industry.

Additionally, corporate America has an attractive, famous, and prestigious Fortune 500 that every American company aspires to belong. The Fortune 500 publishes names of the corporations that are doing well each year regarding revenues and profits in the United States. These businesses are like the cream of the crop; they are among the best ranking of companies by revenues in America, and the annual listing of Fortune 500 companies is published in the Fortune 500 magazine and other major publications.[3]

Business Organization and Ownership

Ownership of business in the United States of America is not a complicated process requiring daunting efforts. Business organization consists of well-structured categories of particular classifications that are independent of one another. Therefore, there are different types of business organizations as well as different forms of business ownerships in the United States. Each of the classifications is unique and mutually exclusive, as is also the case with the ownerships.

Types of Business Organization

Sole proprietorship. How would you like to own your own business? Be your own boss and share the profit and loss to yourself; so, you are not answerable to anyone else? The sole proprietorship is a single-owner business that offers these benefits and much more. If Lisa starts a catering business out of her home and takes no formal legal action to organize in another form, Lisa's business will be a sole proprietorship.

Formation of a sole proprietorship. The sole proprietorship is one of the easiest types of business organizations to form. For example, Lisa, as mentioned above, can start up her catering business by just deciding that she needs to open a catering business in her neighborhood, and may begin to tell her friends about her new venture. She may not need to register her new business with the government. By law, she requires not doing that; all she needs is her willingness and ability to set up and manage her business as a single owner to make profits.

Capital formation. In this example, Lisa may begin to raise capital for her catering business by using her previous savings or borrowing from friends and relatives. For example, Lisa may set aside about $5,000 for starting her catering business. This amount, capital is restrictively set aside, and used to pay the rent, utilities, and food for the catering business. Lisa could as well plan to borrow this money from the bank, except that borrowing from the bank may pose an initial problem for Lisa, since the bank would charge interest on the amount borrowed. The cost to borrow money from the bank and other outside lenders is interest.

Management of a sole proprietorship. Managing the sole proprietorship by oneself is one of the primary advantages of individual ownership of a business. Since Lisa owns the business, she makes all the business decisions by herself without any help from any other person. Lisa decides how much food to cook each day based on her personal knowledge and experience. As a private owner, Lisa shares the profit and loss with no one else and bears the risk of loss by herself. Should Lisa owe anyone while running her catering business, she would also handle paying all the business debts by herself.

Partnership. Sometimes a husband and wife, or two or more friends, classmates, or business associates may contribute money together to engage in a business transaction for profit. This type of business organization is a partnership. The definition of a general partnership is the association of two or more persons to carry on as co-owners of a business for profit. If Judy finds that her fried rice often shows up at catered dinners along with Kate's fruit salads, she may propose to Kate that they join hands to offer a catering service with a full menu and share the profits. If Judy and Kate take no formal legal action to organize in another form, their new business will be a general partnership. If the partnership suffers financial reverses, Judy and Kate are both potentially responsible for paying its debts out of their own individual pockets. If the business profits, it will increase Judy's and Kate's income tax for the year. Whether distributed or not, profits are allocated and taxable directly to the partners. Although previous law treated partnerships as merely an aggregation of partners, current law recognizes the partnership as an entity for most purposes.

Formation of a partnership. The partnership is another form of business ownership that is easy to build. A husband and wife may form a partnership business without any other effort beyond their agreement, since the formation of a partnership business requires only the meeting of minds of two or more people. Nevertheless, because of potential misunderstandings, the partners may choose to register the partnership with the State Registrar Office as a guide to deal with any misunderstanding that might arise in the future concerning the agreement of the partners in relation to the sharing of profit and loss.

Capital formation. The capital formation of the partnership business depends on the mutual agreement of both partners. The partnership agreement contains the amount of the individual interest explicitly. Without partnership registration, the partners may orally agree on how much each of the partners will contribute. For instance, Judy and Kate may decide to register their partnership business or not to register the business. Additionally, Judy and Kate may choose to each contribute $10,000 as capital toward their partnership catering business. The partners need also to agree on how to provide this amount. They may elect to participate equally, $5,000 from each partner, or at any other relative ratio. A significant point to remember about a partnership business is that when the partnership agreement is silent about the ratio of capital contributions and/or when the partners contribute equally, the law requires the partners to share profit and loss equally.

Management of **a partnership.** The management of a partnership business becomes the sole responsibility of the general partner. There are two types of partners—the general partner and the limited partner. The limited partner does not participate in partnership management and is only responsible for his or her initial capital contribution. Furthermore, the limited partner's liability is limited to the initial partner contribution. It is the responsibility of the general partner to manage the partnership business 100 percent of the time and answer to the debts and other liabilities of the partnership business.

Limited Liability Partnership. A limited liability partnership is a partnership with at least one general partner and at least one limited partner. It is different from a general partnership in that its limited partners give up some of the general management rights that partners in a general partnership would have, in exchange for something called limited liability. Thus, if Judy and Kate needed financing for their new catering business, they might ask their wealthy friend Jennet to become an investor. Jennet would not intend to be active in the business and certainly would not wish to become liable for the debts of the catering business. Forming a limited liability partnership would protect Jennet from liability and thereby encourage her to invest her capital. If Jennet took an active role in managing the firm, she would forfeit her limited liability because those who saw her activities would believe her to be a general partner. It bears repeating that a limited liability partnership must have at least one general partner who is liable for the firm's debts. From a legal point of view, a limited liability partnership poses more unnecessary challenges than the other types of business organizations.

Limited Liability Limited Partnership. A limited liability limited partnership (LLLP) is a type of business organization that allows the general partner(s) of a limited partnership to enjoy limited liability, just like the limited partners. Third parties will not be able to force the limited partners or general partners to compensate for the firm's debts. Becoming an LLLP has become much easier under the new law; to elect to become an LLLP, you just need to include a one-line statement to that effect in the certificate of limited partnership. While the other forms of the organizations mentioned in this chapter are common, as of 2014, only about twenty-five states had authorized LLLPs. Note that both general and limited partners in such partnerships would remain liable for the consequences of torts they committed while conducting partnership business. No form of business organization shields people from personal liability for torts they commit.

Limited Liability Company. The organization of a limited liability company (LLC) is gaining momentum in most states as the typical business organization that allows owners limited liability and a single pass-through tax benefit of the partnership form of business ownership. Like the partnership, the LLC is exempt from paying income tax as corporations do. Nevertheless, its profits pass through to each member as subject to individual income tax. The owners are members of the LLC, and each enjoys the right of management, unlike in a partnership, where the general partner manages the daily operating activities of the business. Although there is a uniform statute, the Revised Uniform Limited Liability Company Act (RULLCA), that governs the operations of LLCs, each state has its own legal requirements. In recent years, the majority of new business owners have preferred the LLC as the organizational vehicle.

S Corporation. In corporate America, you can also enjoy operating a business as a corporation with limited liability without paying corporate tax on your corporate profits; rather, the profits transfer to your personal individual income tax liability at the end of the year. The only type of business ownership that offers this kind of organization is the S corporation. A subchapter S corporation can avoid the double taxation that most businesses (called subchapter C corporations) face by meeting certain requirements of subchapter

S of the Internal Revenue Code, including having no more than one hundred shareholders, all of whom unanimously agree to elect subchapter S status.

Formation of an S corporation. As the name implies, an S corporation by law tends to resemble a corporation more than a partnership. A husband and wife may form an S corporation since the formation of an S corporation requires two or more partners, but the current law stipulates that this number of partners may not exceed one hundred. One of the major advantages of an S corporation over the general partnership is the fact that the liability of each of the owners remains limited to the amount of the initial contributions to the S corporation.

Capital formation. An S corporation is one of the types of business organization that encourages each shareholder to contribute toward the capital and still enjoy limited liability by the protection of the law. By law, the owners are the shareholders in the business and not partners as in a partnership. For instance, if Judy and Kate decided to form an S corporation instead of a partnership, the law would protect both Judy and Kate against liabilities and other debts of the business should the business fail. One of the distinctions here is that both shareholders receive immunity from the law and do not face any chastisement by the present and future creditors of the company.

Management of an S corporation. The management of an S corporation does not belong only to a particular shareholder of the S corporation. Each of the shareholders will participate 100 percent of the time in the management of the S corporation based on their previous experiences. The management of an S corporation does not have any restriction on any particular shareholder. The Internal Revenue (IRS) Code of the United States regards the S corporation as a personal holding company.

Corporations

In the United States, there are fifty corporation-chartering states; each of these states uses the word "Inc.", "Corp.", or "Corporation" to denote companies. In some states there are also other suffixes used to identify a corporation, such as "Co." or "Ltd." Some states that allow the use of "Company" do not allow the use of "and Company," "and Co.," or "& Co." A corporation is an artificial legal entity. Its owners (shareholders) typically enjoy limited liability.

The creation of the notion of the artificial legal entity to encourage people to invest in other people's business ideas was one of the great advances in Western legal thought. Judy may buy General Motors stock because she is secure in the notion that even if General Motors goes bankrupt, she will not be liable for its obligations. Her potential loss is limited to the amount she invested when she bought GM stock. Typically, corporations have the burden of double taxation, meaning they pay corporate income tax on their profits, and then when they distribute the dividend to shareholders these shareholders again, pay individual income tax on their dividend income.

Formation of a corporation. Among all the different types of business organizations, the corporation is the most involved to form because of the different documentation requirements. The law looks at a corporation as an artificial person with rights and liabilities. A corporation has absolute power to own properties, can enter into contracts, and has an indefinite life (ad infinitum). Companies do not have any restrictions as to the number of owners as in the case of other forms of business ownership like partnerships or S corporations. Unlimited shareholders can own a corporation. The formation of a company is within the confines of the initial shareholders or the promoters submitting registration documents to the State Registrar's Office. The company should file articles of incorporation and a corporate bylaw stipulating its registered office; in turn, the State Registrar's Office will issue articles of incorporation if it determines that the corporation has a legitimate purpose of existence and meets every legal requirement under the law. The purpose or the objectives of forming the company will determine the type of registration requirements. The promoter should prepare articles of incorporation containing the following:

(a) Name of the company,
(b) Business purpose of the corporation,
(c) The number of authorized issued shares of stock of the corporation and the different classes of shares,
(d) The nature of rights granted to each class of share, and
(e) The number of the initial members of the Board of Directors.

Capital formation of a corporation. There are different types of capital of a company. The capital of the company may be ordinary capital or preferential capital. For instance, the authorized and issued capital may be $100,000,000, divided into $600,000 of ordinary capital and $400,000 of preferential capital. These two different types of capital offer separate rights and benefits to the shareholders. The preferential capital shareholders receive preferential treatment to receive first from the profit and loss of the company, while the ordinary capital shareholders take any leftover after the company meets the needs of the preferred stockholders first.

Management of a corporation. The management of a corporation is a specialized function delegated to the members of the board of directors. Current corporate law requires the members of the board of directors to remain independent of the company. As an independent body, the board assumes the ultimate responsibilities of controlling all major legal requirements of the corporation. The primary responsibilities of the board of directors include appointing officers of the corporation, organizing and conducting periodic corporate meetings, establishing capital requirements and numbers and types of issued shares, and much more. The board of directors also owes fiduciary duties, including loyalty, to the corporation.

Franchise

Franchising is very different from the other forms of business ownership in this chapter. In a franchise, the person called the franchisee pays fees to the owner of the franchise, called the franchisor, to use the firm's business model and brand for a prescribed period, generally on an annual basis. The word *franchise* originates from the Anglo-French *franc*, meaning free. The franchisor is the original owner; the franchise is an alternative to building chain stores to distribute goods, and it avoids investment and accumulating liability as a chain.[4] The franchisor's profitability depends on the success of the franchisees. The franchisee has a greater incentive than a direct employee does because he or she has a direct stake in the business as a stakeholder.

Joint Venture

In corporate America, a joint venture often denotes a general partnership-type relation with less duration. Thus, if Judy and Kate join forces to provide an ongoing full-menu catering business, they have a general partnership. However, if they agreed to work together to provide full-menu service for just a onetime dinner, that would constitute a joint venture. General partnership law governs joint ventures, so the distinction between the two is unimportant for legal purposes.

Branding

We often ask these questions: Why does a customer select one brand over another? What are the reasons that would make an individual customer inclined to choose one brand over another? In this chapter, we will discuss some of these reasons and much more using the Predictive Brand Choice (PBC) model.[5] The PBC uses the prospective predicting method, which does not rely on a brand's past performance or a consumer's purchase history for prediction. The PBC model is a brand measurement and prediction system. This system avoids some of the pitfalls researchers face when using traditional methods of predicting which brand names a buyer will choose.[6] In a mature-declining market, PBC can predict a buyer's choice with more than 90 percent accuracy. The field test to collect data for use by PBC is practical and easy to implement at the point of sale. It consists of two interviews about why the buyer is purchasing and consuming the product. The interview collects data about the buyers' brand knowledge and a list of their most often bought brands in the category. This method predicts the way a consumer chooses or discriminates among available brands. Thus, the strategies used in predicting ethnic neighborhoods (Africans, Chinese, Latino, East European, South East Asian, South Asian, and North Asian). Additionally, branding is one of the three primary features of a consumer product. A brand name may be part of a spoken word, such as Nike's swoosh.[7] A brand may be a manufacturing brand or a store brand. Manufacturing brands often identify major appliances, such as Whirlpool; many food items, such as cornflakes; or automobiles, such as Lexus. A store brand is a brand owned by the individual wholesaler, like Kenwood belonging to Sears Roebuck. Both buyers and sellers benefit from branding. A brand efficiently reduces the amount of time a consumer spends in the store.

Other key benefits of branding are brand loyalty and brand equity. Brand loyalty, as the name suggests, is the degree and extent to which a consumer favors a particular product. Brand equity, on the other hand, refers to both the financial and marketing value in collaboration with a brand in the market[8]—for example, Microsoft, Coca-Cola, Sprint, or Mercedes-Benz. Brand strategies include individual branding and family branding.

Branding emerged as a top management priority in the last few decades due to the growing realization that branding is one of the most precious intangible investments that firms have. Driven in part by the passion of this industry, academic researchers have explored different brand-related topics in recent years, generating scores of articles, research reports, and books. These passions and interest gave birth to brand positioning, brand integration, brand equity measurement, brand growth, and brand management.[9]

Every organization envisaged brand and brand management as a significant management priority. Academic research covered enough of the various studies collectively to increase our knowledge of brands. There are ethical research questions that require resolution in the areas of laws or empirical generalizations. Moreover, there are issues frequently raised by practitioners suggesting that the communications, including our findings, have failed to reach and influence a significant population of consumers.

Types of Branding

Emotional branding. Emotional branding is a critical key to marketing success. As the name implies, emotional branding is a marketing strategy used to target the emotions of particular consumers. The risks posed by this approach attract less attention. Emotional-branding strategies are conducive to the emergence of a doppelganger brand image, defined as a family of disparaging images and meanings about a brand that circulate throughout a modern culture. Emotional branding paradoxically encourages the formation and propagation of doppelganger brand imagery.

A Doppelganger brand. A doppelganger (carbon copy) brand image can undermine the perceived authenticity of an emotional branding story and, thus, the value that the brand provides to consumers. For example, with gasoline, the type of vehicle and engine determine the octane level of an automobile. In the United States and Canada, the octane level is about 4 to 6 lower than elsewhere in the world.[9] The least standard octane level in most areas is 87 for unleaded gasoline, 89 to 90 for premium, and 91 to 94 for super unleaded. The proposal is that rather than merely being a threat to manage, a doppelganger brand image can benefit a brand by providing early warning signs that an emotional branding story is beginning to lose its cultural resonance.

An example of the doppelganger brand image starting to haunt the paradigm of emotional branding is Starbucks coffee. The marketing managers can proactively use the insights gained by analyzing a doppelganger brand image.[11] Succinctly, consumers avoid brand names when their emotional-branding promise is seen as inauthentic, and conversely, those emotional-branding strategies succeed when they can function as an authenticating narrative for consumers' identity. Lastly, a lack of perceived authenticity may not be a primary obstacle for brands that do not seek competitive advantage via emotional branding. A broader variety of brands, consumers, and contexts is still very necessary in this area of knowledge.[12]

The relationship between corporate brand and corporate identity require scholars being sensitive to the factors contributing to the fog surrounding corporate identity. A corporate name involves the conscious decision by senior management to distill and make known the attributes of the organization's identity in the form of a clearly defined branding proposition. This thesis underpins organizational efforts to differentiate, enhance the brand, and communicate with the main stakeholder groups and networks. A brand corporate scheme needs overall corporate commitment to the corporate body from every level of employees. This includes top management fealty and financial support. Thus, the virtues of corporate brands include differentiating, communicating, and enhancing.

In the past, marketing capabilities such as distribution and advertisement were higher-level marketing activities. Financial performance positively influences market performance vigorously and directly. The features of innovation and brand marketing focus on innovation priorities. Innovation includes complication and change, whether in technology companies or other organizations in the global environment.[13] Innovation includes many preconditions that are necessary to pave the way for the enterprise to enhance creative new ideas. These conditions include planning a flexible, broad, and flat organizational structure and a corporate culture based on learning. These are the most significant factors for strengthening innovation.

E-Commerce

E-commerce business (electronic business) is the organized effort of individuals, business, and governments to produce and sell for profit goods and services that satisfy the needs of the society through the facilities available on the Internet.[14] E-commerce may be a business-to-business (B2B) model, a business-to-customers (B2C) model, or a business-to-government (B2G) model. The increasing popularity of open standards in B2B e-commerce demands more generalized trust.[15] Countries' social trust continues to affect the use of open and closed B2B e-commerce. Social trust in a country promotes the use of open B2B e-commerce but impedes the use of closed B2B e-commerce. More importantly, social trust negatively moderates the relationship between a firm's level IT experience and closed B2B e-commerce. There is a significant role of social trust in B2B e-commerce, especially in open e-commerce. Nowadays, the competitive unit in many industries has changed from an individual firm to a whole supply chain. Consider the different types of trust, including contextual transaction trust, ethical trust, genetic trust, technological trust, and organizational trust.[16] Both the consumers and the suppliers need to pay more attention to these driving force. The open B2B e-commerce appears to be the predominant method in the future. Nevertheless, countries with low social trust may eventually find moving toward B2B e-commerce may be harder than expected.

The US Census Bureau's Monthly Retail Trade Survey reports that Internet retail sales for 2014 were $304.91 billion, or 15.4 percent higher than the $264,280 billion sales in 2013.[17] The consequences of customer loyalty in an online business-to-customer (B2C) relationship identifies the 8 Cs—character, contact interactivity, customization, choice, care, cultivation, community, and convenience—that potentially influence e-loyalty, developing criteria to evaluate these forces. Studies have shown that these effects, except convenience, affect e-loyalty. Some data also indicate that e-loyalty has an impact on two customer-related outcomes: word-of-mouth promotion and willingness to pay more. It has become apparent that the eBay reputation system produces noticeable strategic responses from both buyers and sellers.

This chapter discusses a better understanding of online business as we consider the strategies and attitudes of entrepreneurial online retailers. Most researchers focus on established, large firms. This chapter focuses on information in the design of online reputation systems as well as relevant policies in a new, thriving marketplace.

The possibility of easy access to information about products and reaching customers globally created new business opportunities and changed business processes. Development of the e-commerce field is another impressive technological advancement in our modern-day existence. E-commerce technology not only revolutionized the practice of commerce by the addition of the possibility of connecting buyers and sellers in virtual environments for the exchange of goods and services; at the same time, it also necessitated challenges about security, privacy, and legal compliance. For instance, consider the security breaches in the areas of credit card fraud in the most popular retail stores in the United States, such as the Target stores. There were about 60 billion cases of identity theft reported in the United States in 2014. Perhaps, as in every emerging field, the exploration, theorization, and application of knowledge require significant efforts to harness the various avenues by which theory and practice can result in the developmental optimization of the scientific field. Furthermore, this new knowledge also requires substantial efforts to comprehend and document how this understanding influences the political, technological, cultural, and societal systems.

While e-commerce has changed our view of international trade worldwide, it is equally significant for business to assess its consumer belief and customer loyalty in the application and adoption of this emerging new technology. Foreign tourist perceptions toward e-commerce and service quality need continuous review. Tourism and the hotel industry, in particular, are a critical key driver for economic growth in every modern society and a reasonable place to start. Customer satisfaction and consumer belief always influence e-commerce service quality and become the propellant to affect customer loyalty in using websites as a substitute for the traditional method of purchases. The perceived user interface quality, the perceived product or service information quality, the notion of security risks, and the concept of privacy are important determinants of the acceptance of e-commerce service. Nevertheless, the use of e-commerce is more prevalent in corporate America than in most other countries.

The growth of e-business has been very impressive and admirable. The content-based recommendation for electronic commerce dealt with in this chapter is the system used to generate approval of the product that customers may want to buy from the available market. This system adds vendors and an easy-to-find product with the available product. Furthermore, with the association rules mining (ARM) and clustering techniques used to make real-time recommendation systems from the user's transaction data set, we can generate rules for the customer-buying tendency. In addition, based on the customer-purchased product and customer profile, one can make recommendations using the ARM technique, albeit this technique is very time-consuming for large datasets compared to the clustering method. Therefore, the ARM technology is not feasible for a real-time recommendation system. The clustering method is preferable as it mitigates this challenge. Hierarchical clustering (HC), makes partition of an utterly massive data set into a tree of clusters and thus decreases the time required for a real-time recommendation system.

Why Do Businesses Fail?

You may ask, "Why do businesses fail?" Of course, some businesses fail for obvious reasons. Glaringly, the slogan "too big to fail" became a popular and familiar slogan in corporate America in the early 2000s. The preponderance that led to the financial and economic downtowns of 2007 through 2009 gave birth to the above slogan. The stories behind the downfall of major companies like Enron, Tyco, and WorldCom, among others, led the Senate

Committee on Banking and Urban Affairs and the House Committee on Financial Affairs to converge about Enron in 2001.[18]

Enron was an American energy company based in Houston, Texas; but cited as the biggest audit failure. Consequently, the Congress of the United States created the Sarbanes-Oxley Act of 2002, whose purpose was to address a series of perceived corporate misconduct and alleged audit failures to strengthen investor trust in the integrity of the US capital markets. Corporate America is not that playing field or melting pot where individuals, corporate officers, and organizations can circumvent the rules without reprimand. While corporate America thrives on innovation, it equally surrounds itself with stringent laws. To succeed in corporate America requires some basic legal skills.

Business failure may be inevitable irrespective of size. Typically, no company wants to fail, big or small. We can learn from the former *"Big-eight"* accounting firms in the United States. I am sure, the Arthur Andersen accounting firm, the Enron, and others, never expected the failure. The fact is that corporate America resembles a microcosm; you could easily incorporate and make a fortune, or you could quickly lose your investment. One interesting thing about failure in general is that an innovator barely frowns at failure, because failure may lead to the bigger fortune in a technological breakthrough. This is why technocrats regularly converge in Silicon Valley in California and trade new ideas.

This book answers fundamental questions about the dynamics of corporate America. What is innovation? What are the roles and significance of innovation? How can we manage innovation? What is the price of innovation in corporate America? Chapter 1 addresses question 1, while chapter 2 is dedicated to question 2; chapter 3 focuses on question 3, chapter 4 discusses question 4, and chapter 5 discusses question 5. Creativity and innovation are intertwining concepts and the building blocks of corporate America.

While this book may not make you an expert on innovation, it may point you in the right direction. Innovation continues to play a significant role in corporate America. The sustenance of corporate America and the marketplace resonate on recognition of innovation as both the creator and sustainer. Each time engineers in companies like Intel manufacture a generation of computer chips; the company's fortune grows because it has already created the market. This new idea instantaneously compels customers such as IBM, Dell, Toshiba, HP, and other computer producers to satisfy the needs of their customers.[19]

Conversely, innovation also has its drawbacks in corporate America. Organizations need to maintain a competitive edge to remain relevant in today's marketplace. Innovation can even destroy businesses. Many well-known corporations and organizations have gone under because of the advent of new technology. The patterns of large companies, like Walmart superstores and Home Depot/Office Depot/Staples, reconfigure the ranks of small local retailers. Similarly, innovation in new technology, electronics, pharmaceuticals, and other fields continually undermine some known products and services. Unfortunately, businesses and organizations that fail to recognize this pace suffer left behind. Indeed, we are living in exciting times; technology is also winning and revolutionizing information technology (IT) and information systems (IS).

Innovation has become the dominant actor in corporate America, setting the stage for everyone. Of course, that is what actors do. The actors' goal is to establish control and captivate their audience. Similarly, technology acts and performs quickly, and seizes the momentum of our dynamic and changing society. Christensen (2011) argued that one of the innovator's dilemmas is the "mudslide episode". The computer and technological age have predominantly monopolized information systems (IS) as well as IT and captured the attention of the too-big-to-fail businesses around the globe. The primary key pitfalls or disadvantages of technological innovation include its cost, as well as the uncertainty of its initial success or failures. It is also time-consuming, sometimes it requires repeated experimentation, and most of the time it requires sacrifice.

Businesses that focus on technological innovation are highly resilient to failure. Most companies like Best Buy, FedEx, Zap Mail, and Apple accepted the challenges of failure as the opportunity cost of technological innovation; their determination as innovators to succeed, though costly, finally paid off.[20]

In the conundrum of today's technology, it is almost impossible to contend that there is such a thing as focused technology innovation because of the pace and time of new innovative ideas in the new emerging markets. Organizational learning is that area of knowledge within organization theory that studies models and the theory of the process by which an organization learns and adapts. Technical innovation relates to organizational learning because most corporations understand that organizational learning is a continuum of repeatable processes. Improvements in prior experiences become meticulous and strategically implemented. Technological innovation involves a series of product failures by learning why those products failed, which results in improved methods of producing better goods and services. Examples of such a result have been the IBM disk drive industry, Pixar's experiences, Ford Motor Company, and Tesla Motors.[21]

Innovative capacities of SMEs could benefit from R&D cooperation to expand access to external knowledge. R&D cooperation among different-size firms provides more knowledge spillover for the SMEs than the larger firms, thereby stimulating interest in collaboration despite constraints from management expertise and valuable intellectual property protection. Organizations that are fearful of sharing innovation secrets lean toward R&D cooperation with research institutions and universities. The ability to absorb and exploit knowledge spillover from cooperation is essential for small firms to be able to innovate. A quantitative examination of a nationwide innovation survey provides data to confirm a positive correlation between innovation and SMEs' decision to pursue R&D cooperation.

Measuring Innovation

Goal 1: Create a link between areas of knowledge creation and entrepreneurs to get new products and services into the market quicker. Areas of expertise include universities, start-up incubators, and innovation zones. Incubators increase survival rates of start-ups, which create new jobs and innovation. Goal 2: Make it easier for SMEs to sell to big companies. Goal 3: Develop programs that prepare a job-ready workforce for the work that is in demand and necessary for innovation. Goal 4: Link leaders from many types of businesses in the region to attract new investment and implement regionally focused strategies. The focus is on enhancing innovation through partnerships and helping businesses succeed.

In this chapter, I have introduced the dynamics of corporate America and innovation in simplistic terms. There are currently key players in corporate America and a host of other contributing factors that make up the dynamism of corporate America. The ten companies listed in Table 1 of this chapter meet the critical criteria for their selection for 2014; however, this list is always evolving and varies each year based on the same yardstick, as demonstrated by comparing Table 1 and Table 2. Nevertheless, the success of these corporations, as discussed in this chapter, depicts the dynamism of corporate America and innovation.

Lastly, significant good news of corporate America and innovation would be incomplete without the mention of a business model of creating, building, and sustaining breakthrough ventures. If we consider the amazing invention of smartphones, for instance, you'd become amazed about measuring innovation. You may ask, "What is Siri in Apple's apps?" The Stanford Research Institute (SRI) helped invent relevant technologies in corporate America, and others as distinct as in aviation, telecommunications, banking, and aerospace. The "Siri," embedded with artificial intelligence, is a voice-driven "do engine." It understands queries, automatically accesses the data needed, and reproduces them into a spontaneous response.[22] In 2010, Apple launched the Siri device in its iPhone apps. With a push of a button, you receive instant answers to any question posed by voice recognition.

Innumerable other technological advancements are revolutionizing and improving the way we know of doing things in our homes, offices, industries, hospitals, and the marketplace. For instance, some known companies involved in space programs include Boeing, Airbus Group, Lockheed Martin, MacDonald Dettwiler, and Northrop Grumman. These companies also dominate other areas of aerospace, such as the construction of aircraft. The aerospace profession has expanded from hardware-based science, technology, and engineering to systems, and even systems of systems-based engineering.[23] With the demonstrated success of unmanned aerial vehicles (UAVs) for military surveillance and reconnaissance missions and weapons deployment, researchers are envisaging innovative civil and commercial applications for UAVs. Interest is growing in using UAVs for aerial photography, surveying land and crops, monitoring forest fires and environmental conditions, and protecting our borders and ports against intruders. According to the Federal Aviation Administration (FAA), in the United States alone, approximately fifty companies, universities, and government establishments have developed and produced around 155 unmanned aircraft designs.

Before the pinnacle of business travel crashed in 2000, the Concord, considered a marvel of aviation technology, the single droop-nose aircraft that flew at twice the speed of sound, flew from London to New York in less than four hours—half the time of commercial airliners. Boeing, Lockheed Martin, and Aerion are working on another supersonic technology, a supersonic business jet to be in service by the year 2020.[23] These are some measures of innovation in the aviation industry.

Additionally, the banking sector in the United States has indeed evolved into a mobile banking system. People can now make deposits to business and personal accounts with the click of a button from their iPhones. Indeed, the measure of corporate America would be shortsighted without innovation. Thus, innovation is the bedrock of corporate America.

Business Model

There is no consensus on the definition of *business model* in the literature. Each author defines business model differently; however, a business model is the description of how an organization captures, creates, and delivers value.[24] There are distinct building blocks of the business model. These building blocks include

- customer segment,
- value proposition,
- cost structure,
- key partnerships,
- customer relationships,
- primary activities,
- primary resources, and
- revenue streams.

Customer segment. The customer segment is a major building block of a business model. The customer segment constitutes the various individuals, organizations, or groups of people the business plans to serve regarding their needs, attributes, and behavior. Customers are inevitable to any business model. Without profitable customers, no organization can thrive or remain relevant for a long time.

Value proposition. The critical decision every business organization faces is identifying what type of product or service creates value to a particular customer segment. The value proposition is a key factor for why a customer chooses one company over another. A customer in need of a car may prefer Toyota rather than the products of Ford Motor Company. The value proposition is one of the significant building blocks of a business model.

Cost structure. A business model differs from its cost structure. The process of creating and delivering value, generating revenue, and maintaining customer relationships involves costs. The best cost structure requires cost containment. The cost of operation is a derivative of various business segments: primary resources, key partnerships, and major business activities. Therefore, the best cost structure in a business model is a low cost-driven strategy. Cost structure includes all costs inherent in operating a business model.

Key partnerships. Another building block of a business model is creating an alliance with a network of suppliers and noncompeting partners. The different ways to form a key partnership in building a business model include (a) joint ventures, (b) strategic alliances with noncompeting firms, and (c) creating buyer-supplier relationships. The design of a reliable and workable business model includes forming an alliance with critical partners to gain competitive advantages.

Customer relationships. Customer relationships are a key building block of a successful business model. In today's volatile marketplace, a business must define the type of its customer relationships by creating different customer segments. Businesses that negate this cornerstone building block end up struggling with extinction. Some cell phone companies, like Sprint or Verizon, sometimes give free phones or free data to maintain customer relationships. Organizational performance influences customer relationships. The more loyal customers a company maintains, the more profitable the business becomes.

Primary activities. There are inherent activities in every business model. Primary activities are the core actions an organization takes to succeed in a business operation, such as utilizing key resources, determining market participation, enhancing productivity, creating a value preposition, maintaining good customer relationships, and generating more revenues. The nature of a business model determines the primary activities. For a retail giant like Walmart, key activities include supply chain management. For an automobile manufacturer like Toyota, branding and differentiation are key activities.

Primary resources. One of the critical building blocks of a business model is primary resources. All business models require key resources. Therefore, primary resources determine the success and failure of most business models. Key resources include human resources, financial resources, material resources, and technology. For any business model to succeed, the organization should ensure that it has identified the key resources to reach its customers, suppliers, markets, and industry. The type of business model determines the nature of key resources; a large manufacturer requires capital-intensive productive facilities, whereas a small retailer shop would need a less-capital-intensive operating facility.

Revenue streams. Revenue streams are the primary sources of building a block of any business model. Revenue streams represent the physical cash an organization generates from each customer segment. Each customer segment is willing to pay for the value received from the business. This determination is the very essence of every business's existence. What amount are the customers willing to pay for the products or services provided by the business? Revenue streams less the costs incurred is the net earnings; the lower the costs, the higher the profits. The two sources of income include transaction revenues, resulting from onetime customer fixed-list price payments, and recurring revenue from ongoing customer payments as in installment sales.

Corporate Social Responsibility

Corporate social responsibility (CSR) is the corporate initiative to assess and take responsibility for the company's effects on environmental and social well-being. The British Petroleum Company (BP) is one of the largest oil companies in the world based on market capitalization and proven reserves. In most recent years, this corporate giant has continued to sustain various environmental challenges. The BP oil spill of more than 200 million gallons of crude oil into the Gulf of Mexico was one of the biggest in US history.[25] While every business organization faced with financial and environmental challenges, some business risks are overwhelmingly critical. BP paid a finalized settlement of $20.8 billion; the largest financial penalty ever leveled by the US government against a single company.[26] The Company was able to sustain its corporate image by being proactive over its risk averseness and fate in corporate social responsibility (see photos 1–3).

Corporate social responsibility continues to dominate the pages of our newspapers and our social discourse. Most organizational leaders have come to grasp the essence of CSR as an important component of corporate operating expenses. The neglect of this significant corporate responsibility becomes a recipe for corporate failures, leading to endless legal battles. Therefore, CSR represents an indelible cost of owning and operating a business in the twenty-first century. No business, large or small, is immune to the environmental challenges posed by CSR.

Exhibit A:
Civil suit against BP for Gulf oil spill begins.

BP oil spill in the Gulf of Mexico

Exhibit B:
Gulf Coast struggles with oil spill and its economic costs.

BP oil spill in the Gulf of Mexico.

Exhibit C:
Gulf oil spill begins to reach land as BP struggles to contain leak.

Corporate Ladder

According to a US Department of Labor (DOL) News Brief, women earn about eighty cents on the dollar compared to men.[27] Similarly, in the corporate world, there is a divergence in corporate remuneration between the sexes. The current social discussion emphasizes equal pay for all in accordance with the US Title VII Equal Pay Act of 1964, but in reality, males continue to earn more than their female counterparts do. This dominance of inequality places a stigma of social strata in the minds of professional executives. Corporate America is not immune to this dichotomy (see exhibit D.2). The corporate world consists of irresistible competition, and one's position in the professional class stems from value competencies. Sometimes the current position does not depend on academic majors. In corporate America, corporations usually reward their employees based on competencies. Therefore, climbing the corporate ladder depends on an individual's skills and competitiveness. If an employee can demonstrate the skill and ability to give measurable value to the corporation's goals and objectives—maximizing profit—the corporate ladder becomes accessible and attainable.

Exhibit D
Corporate ladder—1.

Exhibit E:
Corporate ladder—2.

The Fair Labor Standard Act of 1938 (FLSA) regulates employment in America. FLSA introduced the 40 hours work week and established the national minimum wage and guarantteed a time and half for overtime in certain jobs.[28] The FLSA applies to any employee employed by an employer but not independent to independent contractors or volunteers since they are not considered employees under the FLSA.[29] Further, the FLSA applies to employees who are engaged in interstate commerce or in the production of goods for commerce, or who are employed by an enterprise engaged in commerce or in the production of goods for commerce. The Equal Pay Act of 1963 ameded te FLSA.[30] In Corporate America, the employee's skills and competencies are the criteria and core determinants of levels of positions on a Corporate Ladder. The public sector on the other hand uses the merit system for recritment. The minimum wage is the base of earning legally paid for unsckilled work. Currently, this amount has been subjected to political expediency, and contoversy. Only the United States of America Congress has the legal authorization to establish the amount of minimum wage. At the time writing this book, the amount of minimum wage is $7.50/hour. However, the political discuss today is to raise this amout to adjust for inflation.

The Securities Stock Exchange Commission

The Security Exchange Commission – the Securities Exchange Act of 1934, created the SEC. As an agency of the federal government of the United States of America, it regulates the federal securities laws. It holds primary responsibility for enforcing the federal securities laws, proposing securities rules, and regulating the securities industry, the nation's stock and options exchanges, and other activities and organizations, including the electronic securities markets in the United States.[31] The Securities Act of 1934 regulates new securities; whereas, the Securities Act of 1933, regulates existing securities. The SEC was created by Section 4 of the Securities Exchange Act of 1934 (now codified as 15 U.S.C. § 78d and commonly referred to as the Exchange Act or the 1934 Act).[32]

Major Stock Exchanges in the United States

The three primary stock exchanges in the United States include the following:

(a) the New York Stock Exchange, (NYSE) - The New York Stok Exchange is the world's largest security market with listed companies of $19.69 trillion as of May 2015.32 The NYSE founded in May 17, 1792.

(b) National Association of Securities Dealers Automated Quotation System

(NASDAQ) – As the term suggests, NASDAQ is a global electronic marketplace for buying and selling securities, as well as the standard for index for the U.S. technology stocks. The national association of securities dealers (NASD) created this type of securities to enable investors to trade securities on a Computerized Speedy and Transparent System (CS&TS).

The system began operation on February 8, 1971. There are more than 3000 stocks listed on the Nasdaq composite exchange, which includes the world's famous technology and biotechnology giants such as Apple, Google, Microsoft, oracle, Amazon, and Intel.

(c) American Stock Exchange (AMEX) – Unlike NASDAQ and NYSE, AMEX focuses on the exchange of Traded Funds (ETFs).[33]

Table 4, discloses the top 10 largest stocks by market capitalization, with Apple, Inc. with the highest market capitalization of $546.8 billion, and China Mobile Ltd., with the list stock capitalization of $246.7 billion in January 2016.

Table 1.
The Top Ten Largest US Corporations by Revenue and Employment—2014

Ranking	Name	Industry	Revenue in (USD millions)	No. Employees
1	Wal-Mart Store, Inc.	Retail	$476, 294	2.2 Million
2	Exxon	Oil and gas	411,939	76,900
3	Chevron	Oil and gas	211,970	64,700
4	Berkshire Hathaway	Conglomerate	194,673	316,000
5	Apple	Electronics	182,795	80,300
6	General Motors	Automotive	155,929	284,000
7	General Electric	Conglomerate	148,589	307,000
8	Ford Motors	Automotive	144,007	164,000
9	Valero Energy	Oil and gas	130,844	10,000
10	Philips 66	Oil and gas	130,180	13,500

Source: *Fortune 500 (2014).*

Table 2:
The Top Ten Largest US Corporations by Revenue and Employment—2013

Ranking	Corporation Name	Industry	Revenue $ million	No Employees
1	Exxon Mobile	Energy	454,926	99,100
2	Wal-Mart Stores	Retail	445,950	2,200,000
3	Chevron	Energy	245,621	61,189
4	ConocoPhillips	Energy	245,621	29,800
5	General Motors	Automobile	150,476	202,000
6	General Electric	Diversified	147,616	301,000
7	Berkshire Hathaway	Diversified	143,688	288,500
8	Fannie Mae	Finance	137,451	7,300
9	Ford Motor	Automobile	136,264	164,000
10	Hewlett-Packard	Computer	127245	350,610

Source: Fortune 500, 2013

Table 3:
The Top Ten Largest US Banks by Assets—2012

Ranking	Bank Name	Assets $ million	No. Employees	Profit $ million
1	JP Morgan Chase	2,359,000	258965	21,280
2	Bank of America	2,209,000	276,600	4,188
3	Citigroup	1,865,000	259,000	7,415
4	Wells Fargo	1,422,000	265,000	18,890
5	Goldman Sachs	923,220	57,726	7,475
6	Morgan Stanley	749,890	57,726	(117)
7	Bank of NY Mellon	359,301	48,700	2,569
8	U.S. Bancorp	353,000	62,529	5,600
9	HSBC North American Holdings	318,801	43000	n/a
10	Capital One Financial	286,602	35,593	3,517

Source: Fortune, 2012

Table 4
10 Largest Stocks by Market Cap - 2016

Company Symbol	Sector	Industry	Prior Close	5 Day Change %	4 Week Change %	52 Week Change %	Market Cap Billions
AAPL Apple Inc.	Technology	Computers, Phones, & Household Electronics	99.83	2.94	4.97	-22.98	546.8
MSFT Microsoft Corp.	Technology	Software & IT Services	53.96	2.61	7.77	15.74	424.2
XOM Exxon Corp.	Energy	Oil & Gas	94.82	0.99	4.06	14.78	393.2
AMZN Amazon.Com Inc.	Consumer Cyclicals	Diversified Retail	736.07	-2.35	3.09	52.39	347.3
FB Facebook Inc.	Technology	Software & IT	119.37	1.27	5.29	25.69	349.48
JNJ Johnson & Johnson	HealthCare	Pharmaceuticals	123.14	0.17	5.66	23.04	338.7
GE General Electric Co.	Industrials	Industrial Conglomerates	32.91	2.17	6.75	20.81	302.6
T AT & T Inc.	Telecommunication Services	Telecommunication Services	42.85	0.80	5.08	22.39	263.8
GOOGLE Alphabet Inc.	Technology	Software & IT Services	753.20	3.58	6.67	7.66	258.4
CHL China Mobil Ltd. (ADR)	Tele-communication Services	Telecommunication Services	60.25	4.82	8.48	-4.21	246.7

Source: Scottrade, (2016)

Figure 2.1
The circular flow model.

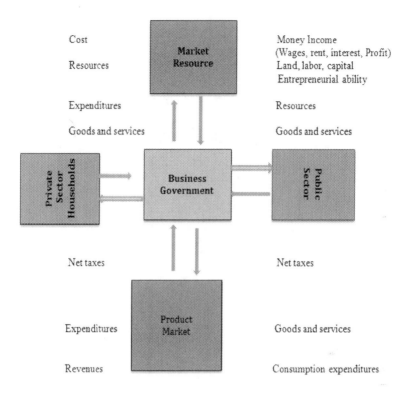

Figure 2.2
The dynamics of corporate America

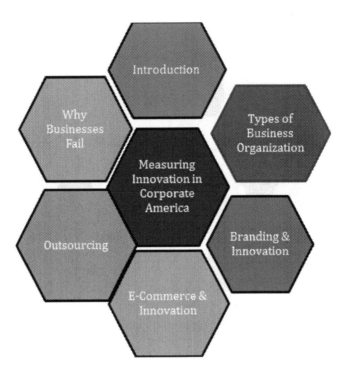

Figure 2.3
The elements of a business model

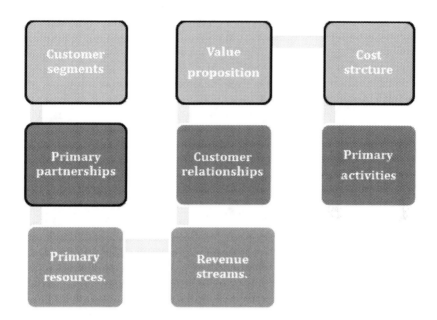

Chapter 3

The Role of Innovation in Corporate America

*If your actions inspire others to dream more, learn more, do more,
and become more, you are a leader.*
—John Quincy Adams

*The question I ask myself like almost every day is, "Am I doing the
most important thing I could be doing?" ... Unless I feel like I'm
working on the most important problem that I can help with, then
I am not going to feel good about how I'm spending my time. And
that's what this company is.*
—Sam Walton, CEO of Walmart

Innovation and strategy are intertwining tools used by organizational leaders to plan and implement transformational change in any particular organization. Whereas innovation breeds and feeds on new ideas, strategy fashions the hatched ideas into a product or service. Therefore, in corporate America, innovation is the pivot upon which the wheels of business management thrive. The application of these twin factors in any organization yields increased positive results. Innovation will continue to promote creativity in an organization. Similarly, strategy in the hands of organizational leaders motivates innovation toward a constructive and profitable product or service. Hence, there is a symbiotic relationship between innovation and strategy.

As declared by the National Council on Competitiveness in 2005, in short, if America stopped innovating, we would stop being Americans.[1] In corporate America, innovation to an extent is the result of an interactive process of knowledge mining, application, and diffusion. The significance of knowledge interactions for innovation continues to challenge today's managers. Thus, the concepts of knowledge spillovers, innovation networks, and innovation systems are critical and equally important business management tools. Accordingly, the innovation systems model brings in different actors; the science sector, the business sector, and policy actors are all involved in the process. The various kinds of innovation, like radical or advanced innovations, rely on unique knowledge sources. More often than not, these types of knowledge sources come from universities and research organizations. Incremental innovations, on the other hand, take place more often in the interaction among different partners and business associates.

From the time Thomas Edison invented the electric lightbulb in 1878 until now, the quest for innovation in corporate America has continued to intensify. Innovation has been the bedrock of transformational knowledge in human history.[2] The technological advancement of the last thirty to fifty years created the need for this book. The ten highest valued technical companies in corporate America today are (1) Apple, (2) Google, (3) IBM, (4) Samsung, (5) Microsoft, (6) AT&T, (7) General Electric, (8) Vodafone, (9) Intel, and (10) HP. These conglomerates lead the way by deciding the price we pay for their products in today's market.[3] Innovation continues to give credence to new knowledge and new ideas. More-efficient devices, novelty, new products, new markets, discovery, and new gadgets influence our regular daily routine and way of life. Innovation continues to be one of the most useful tools ever known to man.

Often, we perceive a word based on its roots; *innovation* has a Latin origin of *nova*, meaning new. Katz defined innovation as the embodiment, combination, or synthesis of knowledge in an original, relevant, valued new product, process, or service.[4] Historically, George Baldwin invented the first gasoline automobile in 1876; the Wright Brothers invented the first airplane in 1903 in the United States. In 1886 a pharmacist named John Pemberton created Coca-Cola in the United States. Today, daily servings of Coca-Cola are about 1.9 billion worldwide.[5] The navigation devices based on global positioning satellite (GPS) technology found in many luxurious automobiles and electronic stores owe less to innovation than to the application of existing GPS technology to a new use. Some of us know what life used to be like over twenty years ago and how well some of us drove around the main cities and states before GPS. Of course, some of these new inventions and innovations seem to add a bit of paradox with our dependence on them. Sometimes dependency on some of these new technologies affects our natural instincts and causes loss of memories. With the introduction of smartphones, I can barely remember people's telephone numbers and addresses anymore without my cell phone. Sometimes it is hard to determine whether such dependency is healthy for our human minds.

The Internet is another outstanding innovation. In fact, this invention has remarkably transformed and revolutionized our human experience. The Internet has affected every spectrum of human endeavor globally. No wonder some experts argue that the world has become a global village. The irony of it all is that to become an active participant and thrive in this new arena, you must determine to give yourself to lifetime learning. Sometimes it seems that our world has become a conundrum of increased knowledge; for instance, before you finish assembling the newest gadget you purchased, be it an iPhone or a laptop, another new model is already out in the market. Thank goodness, for our children, who are indeed a blessing; the best part is that they, in turn, have become the technocrats and recommendable coaches to most parents. Imagine the time and dedication of these children to master the quagmire and barrage of new technology.

Technological Obsolescence

The irony of technology is the nature of obsolescence. Some technical inventions easily become obsolete, and their obsolescence poses difficulties to consumers. Let me begin with the disk drive, the typewriter, data processing equipment, and mainframe computers. These types of technology worked and operated efficiently during their technological feasibility span, but have now given way to more modern technology. Innovation is the key to the transformational changes in technology. Before the iPhone, compare what life used to be like with the palm-size smartphones with seemingly endless features, phones like Motorola's RAZR, which peaked with its embedded camera. Mobile phones have a long history. Alexander Graham Bell's invention of the telephone in 1876 was a highlight in the era of talking at a distance.[6] In the twentieth century, innovators expanded the telephone's reach across continents, shrinking the world and connecting its citizens. Electronic switching systems enabled customers to make phone calls without the assistance of operators. Using cellular technology, by the end of 2010, more than 5.3 billion people all over the world had gone wireless.[7] Today, there are approximately 150 million subscribers worldwide. The cellular industry generates $30 billion in annual revenues and is one of the fastest growing industries.[8]

In the 1900s, telephone transmission extended across and between the main cities. As telephone communication reached across and between the main towns, there was the insertion of loading coils along the lines to reduce distortion. The first transcontinental phone came to fruition in 1915. In 1919, the switching systems and rotary-dial telephone came on board from Bell Atlantic. Then in 1949, the AT&T presented the first phone to combine a ringer and handset.[9] The first direct long-distance phone call entered the United States in 1951. In 1963 came the first touch-tone phone. In 1973 Martin Cooper, of Motorola, introduced the first portable cell phone. By the end of 2007, there were 295 million subscribers on 3G networks worldwide.[10] During this time, the two key distributors were the American Telephone, Telegraph Company (AT&T) and Bell Atlantic; they predominantly monopolized the telecommunication market.

Innovative ideas may come from varied sources. They may come as inspiration or mere imagination. Over fifty years ago, the computer was not popular in our local markets. Thomas Edison once said that invention is 99 percent perspiration and 1 percent inspiration.[10] This chapter provides an overview of innovation and corporate America in the last fifty years. In corporate America and today's global marketplace, the quest for new ideas will continue to persist.

Innovative ideas may evolve from new ideas, customers, new knowledge, empathetic design, lead users, open market of ideas, skunkworks, and innovation laboratories. The designation *skunkworks* used widely in business, engineering, and technical fields to describe a group within a company given a high degree of autonomy, unhampered by bureaucracy, tasked with working on advanced or secret projects.

This chapter further discusses the significant role of mental preparedness, which organizational leaders could use to generate additional good ideas. Some organizations have made protracted management decisions to encourage the generation of concrete business ideas. Note that in this environment, no idea is wrong or tossed out without going through the normal processing.

Innovation and Its Challenges

Xerox Corporation, the leading copier company, had a storied history of innovation. Some of this innovation arose from Xerox's Palo Alto Research Center (PARC), which aimed at creating a new market for the Xerox computer industry. Only a few people knew the whole story of Xerox's problems of capturing value from such massive investments in innovation at PARC.[12] In 1969 Jacob Goldman, the head of the Xerox company, embarked on innovating the PARC project to make Xerox the architect of information, which would transform Xerox from the leading office copier to the office supplier of information. The PARC project failed after thirty years.

Xerox's experience with PARC raises questions: How could a company that possessed the resources and vision to launch a brilliant research center—not to mention the patience to fund the center for thirty years and the savvy to incorporate important technologies from it—let so many good ideas get away? Did Xerox mismanage PARC? Why did so much of PARC's computer industry innovation yield so little for Xerox and its shareholders? The cause of Xerox's PARC failure based on the way Xerox managed its innovation process. Xerox achieved PARC through a closed innovation paradigm instead of an open innovation paradigm.[13] The corporation sought to discover new breakthroughs; develop them into products; make the products in its factories; and distribute, finance, and service those products—all within the four walls of the company. This paradigm was the leading industrial R&D technology used to manage facilities operating in corporate America after World War II; it was hardly unique to Xerox.[14]

The Process of Innovation

Recognizing opportunity is the process when a team player says, "This invention may be of value to customers" or "I wish we could solve this problem that could create value for clients and shareholders equally". The idea becomes more meaningful when management discovers that such an approach might reduce cost.

After recognizing the opportunity phase, the incubation of the same idea begins attracting the evaluation process by decision makers. Solutions must be expanded to provide answers to the following questions:

(a) Does the company possess the expertise to bring the idea to fruition?
(b) Is the idea workable?
(c) Is the idea cost effective?
(d) Does the idea create value to customers?
(e) Is the idea corporate strategy?

Ideas ranked on predetermined criteria and analyzed, and the ideas with affirmative responses and that receive management support move to the commercialization phase.

In this process, creativity controls initiated and improve the ideas as they move forward. Nowadays innovation is an interactive process of knowledge generation and application. The business sector, the science sector, and policy areas are involved in the process, as stressed in concepts such as innovation systems and the network approach. To what extent do different kinds of innovation rely on specific knowledge sources and links? Succinctly, more advanced innovations, on the one hand, might draw more on scientific knowledge, generated in universities and research organizations. Incremental changes and the adoption of new technologies, on the other hand, seem to occur often in integration with partners from the business sector and at higher spatial levels. Furthermore, firms introducing innovation that is more advanced rely to a larger extent on R&D and patents, and they cooperate more often with research organizations and universities.[15]

Types of Innovation

The traditional categorization of innovation as either incremental or radical is incomplete and potentially misleading; it did not account for the sometimes disastrous effects on the industry incumbents of seemingly minor improvements in technological products.[16] There is innovation that changes the core design concepts of technology and innovation that changes only the associations among them. Hence, innovation comes in different shapes and forms. Obviously, however, innovation is the lifeblood of corporate America.

Architectural innovation. As the name implies, architectural innovation changes only relationships within the product architecture but leaves the component and the core design concepts that they embody unchanged. Architectural innovation presents established companies with a more elusive challenge—for example, the semiconductor precise alignment equipment industry. Modular innovation changes the core design concepts of technology, such as the replacement of analog with digital telephones. The fact that one can replace an analog dialing device with a digital one is an example of innovation that changes a core design conception without changing the product architecture.[17]

Radical innovation. As stated above, innovation is the embodiment, combination, or synthesis of knowledge in an original, relevant, valued new product, process, or service. The two primary forms of innovation are radical and incremental innovation. Radical innovations are by-products of new knowledge; they emanate from something new to humankind but maintain a distinguishing feature of existing technology. A Harvard professor, Christensen, describes technical innovation that can restructure the existing status quo of organizations and uses the popular name radical or disruptive technology. The digital imaging technology used in consumer and professional cameras revolutionized the coated film technology established by George Eastman over the centuries. In corporate America, these two forms of innovation concept are predominantly interchangeable.

Incremental innovation. Incremental innovation exploits already existing technologies by changing their forms. The GPS is a typical example of incremental innovation.

Service innovation. In corporate America, consumer satisfaction determines organizational performance; hence, service becomes a significant area of concern. Companies make more profit and stay in business longer when they meet the needs of their customers. For example, Southwest Airline's, HP's, and Dell Computers' service meet high quality standards. Service innovation is taking extra steps to create new ideas on how to improve customer service as well as treat a customer like a king. In corporate America, creating a brand name and providing quality service are the key to longevity.

Product innovation. A product innovation is a new technology or combination of technologies introduced to meet user need. New product and process technologies to date have been descriptive to identify consistent patterns in the sources of idea usage, message processes, and characteristics of successful innovation.[15] Product innovation provides an added technological advancement in today's organization.

Disruptive innovation. Disruptive innovation is more prevalent in the automobile industry. Toyota, for instance, explored the American auto industry with its first Corona, but the auto markets had become predominantly saturated with electric cars. Disruptive innovation results when new technology restructures a product based on the emerging needs of target customers. In all likelihood, the demand for electric cars was prevalent in US markets because of their cost advantage, simplicity, and reliability.

Industry and Marketing Leadership

Product, service, and cost differentiation. The three generic strategies for achieving above-average performance in competitive corporate America are cost leadership, differentiation, and focus. For example, there is Caterpillar Tractor's differentiation based on product durability; for Japanese car manufacturers like Toyota and Honda, fuel efficiency and hybrid vehicles are the norm. In corporate America, it is one thing to create an innovative new product, but another thing to establish a process capable of producing it at a price to attract the target market. Procter & Gamble (P&G) challenged General Foods' Maxwell House brand, but P&G's Folger's had little or no product superiority over Maxwell House. Using the same value chain as General Foods, P&G produced and marketed Folger's coffee; however, Maxwell House retaliated by a broad array of defensive tactics, benefiting from its established market share and favorable cost position. When P&G started, its R&D department quickly solved the performance problem using materials that were more suitable in design. The problem was creating a cost-effective process for producing its new diapers. Succinctly, the challenge was creating the production process, not developing a product new idea.

In this chapter, my focus has been to explore the positive impact of sustainable innovation management in corporate America. Particular areas of further research on the topic are critical to investigate this phenomenon. There are other specific areas to explore such as conducting a study to examine the negative impact of sustainable innovation management and determine the level of such adverse effects on growth and profitability in corporate America. Another specific research study area may include investigating the information-age technology and its championed postindustrial revolution. Such study would reposition innovation management and environmental sustainability. There are four goals to spur innovation in corporate America:

(1) To create a link among areas of knowledge;
(2) To create entrepreneurs able to get new products and services into the market even quicker than just in time (JIT);
(3) The areas of knowledge include universities, start-up incubators, and innovation zones;
(4) Incubators increase survival rates of start-ups that create new jobs and change.[18]

Further, innovation will make it easier for small firms to sell to big companies. Additionally, to develop programs that prepare a job-ready workforce for work that is in demand and necessary for innovation; and lastly, to link leaders from many types of businesses in the region to attract new investment and implement regionally focused strategies. The goals focus on enhancing innovation through partnerships and helping small businesses succeed.

Innovation management. Innovation management includes a set of tools that allow managers and engineers to cooperate with a shared understanding of goals and processes. Therefore, innovation management enables the organization to respond to opportunities by using its creativity to enhance new ideas, processes, or products. Significantly, innovation management should involve workers at every level in contributing creatively to an organization's development, manufacturing, and marketing. By utilizing appropriate innovative management tools, management triggers and deploys the creative ingenuity of the whole workforce toward the development of the organization.

This process is an evolutionary integration of the organization, technology, and market by integrating a series of activities: search, select, capture, and implement. Therefore, sustainable innovation management helps firms to harness their competencies and gain competitive advantage. The understanding of information technology (IT) enables organizations to use necessary technology in a proactive manner to create value for their stakeholders and spur innovation. Moreover, as business transforms to be knowledge-based, innovation management also ensues. Competing in overcrowded industries is no way to sustain high performance; the real opportunity is to create a niche of uncontested market space. That will create demand rather than fight over it, and many opportunities for growth that will be both profitable and rapid. Those organizations that accept taking advantage of these new ideas and reverse their business models will beat the odds.

The concept of evolutionary advantage continually surfaces new currents in the world of business; however, the static positional advantage offered by classical Portenian analysis is no longer sufficient. The emerging direction of business strategy, and its first major forms of business knowledge over the last century, is the mainstream frameworks for strategic analysis, and offered, as a compelling alternative, the emerging notions of evolutionary development and transformative learning.[19]

Most businesses depend on others for their success. Such a business practice spells significant strategic implications—timing is usually affected; under the network, a firm getting to market ahead of its rivals would only be of value if the partners were also ready. Indeed, the organizational selection process of innovation and assessing the interdependency risks of coordinating with complementary innovators may not answer the question "Whose projects must succeed first?" Moreover, when benefits do not exceed costs at every adoption step, intermediaries will not move offering the line.[18]

Sustainable innovation management. In this chapter, my focus has been to explore the role of innovation in corporate America, discussing technological obsolescence, innovation and its challenges, the process of innovation, types of innovation, competitive advantage, sustainable innovation management, and research and development in corporate America. The primary objective is to discover the role technology plays in corporate America. Sustainable innovation requires a team effort of the management, employees, and other stakeholders.[20] Thus, innovation management depicts activities, decisions, and practices that elevate an idea to the realization for generating business value. Innovation management relates to managing the investment in creating new opportunities for generating customer values that can sustain the growth of the organization. Innovation management focuses on the development of services, products, or technologies. Nevertheless, the types of innovation that can enhance business results go well beyond these, including changes to the company's business model. Identifying and making business investments successfully and repeatedly constitutes the primary objective of innovation management.

In today's information age, in a globalized marketplace, sustainable innovation management is pivotal for the significance of small-medium enterprises (SMEs). The growth and profitability of this sector are incumbent on continued implementation of new ideas in information management. Most SMEs failed to implement technology-based tactics to build their businesses. Interestingly enough, the information age is vociferous and ubiquitous, revolutionizing business management, as well as providing new ideas for maximizing business growth and profitability for SME. Knowledge management has contributed immensely to the continued growth and development of SMEs. Firms that fail to adopt the implementation of technology-based tactics to build their businesses will struggle with extinction.

Research and development. The linear model of innovation postulates that innovation starts with basic research, followed by applied research and development, and then production and diffusion. The linear model is the first theoretical framework developed for a historical understanding of science and technology. The linear model of innovation was not a spontaneous invention arising from the mind of one individual.[21] There are dual roles of R&D, correcting the misconceptions of many economists. R&D not only generates new information but also enhances the firm's ability to assimilate and exploit existing information. Recognition of the dual role of R& D suggests that the ease and character of understanding within an industry will both affect R&D expenditure and conditions that influence its appropriability and the technological conditions on R&D. Concerning R&D incentives for licensing a production technology and the impact of licensing on the pattern of innovation and its evolution of industry costs and market structure, the gains from trading information via licensing contracts are achieved through the auxiliary of inefficient production techniques. Licensing stimulates innovation when the industry variation in costs is small, but leads to less innovation and possibly higher market prices when costs are asymmetric.[22]

Figure 3.1
The role of innovation

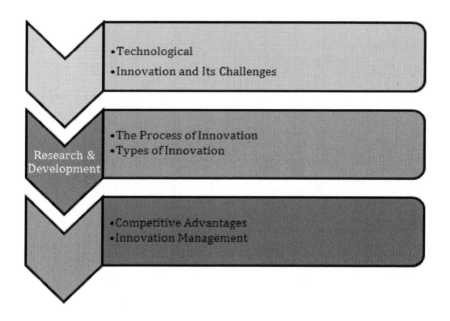

Figure 3.2
The process of innovation

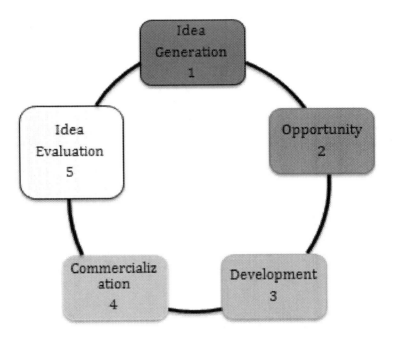

Figure 3.3
Timeline of incremental and radical improvement

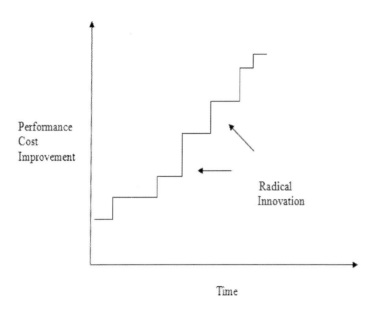

Source: *Managing Creativity and Innovation – HBR* (2003)

Chapter 4

Global Supply Chain

It is amazing what you can accomplish if you do not care who gets the credit.
—Harry S. Truman

There's an entrepreneur right now, scared to death, making excuses, saying, "It's not the right time just yet." There's no such thing as a good time. I started an apparel manufacturing business in the tech-boom years. I mean, come on. Get out of the garage and go take a chance, and start your business.
—Tim Cook, CEO of Apple

In corporate America, supply chain management (SCM) facilitates innovation and increases organizational performance. The definition of SCM is a set of synchronized decisions and activities utilized to efficiently integrate customers, retailers, transporters, warehouse, manufacturers, and suppliers so that the right product or service is distributed in the right quantities, at the right time, to the right location in order to minimize system-wide costs while satisfying customer service level requirements.[1] Supply chain management is one of the fastest and the most proficient methods of running a business. Just in time, (JIT) and lean manufacturing play significant roles in the better functioning of SCM. Some of the lean manufacturing principles include JIT supplier relation principles, JIT inventory principle, JIT production principle, JIT human resource principles, and JIT quality principle.[2] The partnership model was an ideal model to rekindle the supply chain relationship between Wendy's International and Tyson Foods in the United States. The two companies vividly remembered their previous disagreements and chose to move forward in forming a more strategic partnership alliance because of their mutual business interests and changes in administrative positions that consumers' tastes had shifted to favor demand for chicken as opposed to beef.

Supply chain management (SCM) is the organization of the flow of goods and services around a country or the world. The supply chain plays a tremendous role in the movement and storage of raw materials, work-in-progress inventory, and finished goods from point of origin to point of consumption.[3] It covers the interconnectedness or interlinked networks, channels, and nodes of business involved in the process and provision of products and services required by customers in the supply chain. Different authors and researchers have given supply chain management different definitions. Nonetheless, supply-chain definition always includes planning, design, execution, control, and monitoring of supply chain activities to create worth, build competitive infrastructure, leverage worldwide logistics, synchronize demand and supply, and measure their global implications.[4] A supply chain categorically arranges in various stages of networks the following: (a) Type 1 supply chain—systems such as production, storage, distribution, and material control are not linked and are independent of each other. (b) Type

2 supply chain—systems at this stage become integrated into one plan via the enterprise resource planning (ERP); (c) Type 3 supply chain—the achievement of vertical integration with downstream consumers and upstream suppliers.

Historical Overview

The concept of the world becoming a global village and the globalization era contributed immensely to the development of SCM. As the world continued to become smaller and smaller, with emerging globalization influence, the need for large-scale changes, downsizing, and reengineering, facilitated by cost-reduction programs, brought widespread attention to some international management practices. There was also the introduction of the electronic data interchange (EDI) in the 1960s and introduction of enterprise resource planning (ERP). In the late 1980s, many leaders of corporate America began to integrate comprehensive sources into their primary core businesses. The primary goal and objective of SCM is to increase competitive advantage, add value, and reduce cost globally. Corporate America began to focus on specialization and core competencies in the 1980s to 1990s. The wake of this period witnessed the neglect of vertical integration and outsourcing of those functions to partners.

Thus, the specialization model resulted in manufacturing and distribution networks composed of various individual supply chains specific to suppliers, producers, and consumers that came together to manufacture, design, distribute, market, sell, and service products. The introduction of transportation brokerages, warehouse management, on-assets-based carriers, and advanced technologies into the aspect of supply planning collaboration and execution of performance management. This specialization within the SCM-enabled corporate America to expand their overall competencies in the same way that outsourced manufacturing and distribution done, allowing them to specialize in their core competencies and create networks of particular, best-in-class partners to contribute to the overall value chain, thereby increasing overall performance and efficiency.

Agility in Supply Chain Management

The best supply chains are not just fast and cost-effective; they are also adaptable.[5] Moreover, they ensure that all the firms' interests remain intact and unaltered. In the early 1990s, American apparel companies were able to utilize the system to promote the Quick Response Initiative (QRI) in the grocery businesses in Europe; and the United States touted a program called Efficient Consumer Response (ECR) that included the US food service industry, which embarked on an Efficient Food Service Response (EFSR) program.[6]

In the triple-A supply chain, the merits of SCM include considering the effects on individual companies during the economic downturn. SCM offers a competitive advantage to the trading partners during economic slowdowns. The operating efficiency of companies such as Walmart, Dell, and Amazon and their competitive edge over their competition is remarkable. The triple-A supply chain model indicates three distinctive qualities of top-performing supply chains, which is they are agile, adapt, and align the interests of all the firms in the supply network. With the three A's (agility, adaptability, and alignment), Seven-Eleven Japan (SEJ)—a $21 billion convenience store chain—was able to stay ahead of its competition because of the application of this model; SEJ was the world's most profitable retailer. The company's motto and message to its partners were clear: make the business successful and share the rewards, fail to deliver on time and pay a penalty.[7]

China became a major player in global auto manufacturing, and the Chinese auto market provided huge opportunities to manufacturers, suppliers, and service providers. The Chinese market became attractive to most automakers like Toyota, whose fourth joint venture plant produced up to 335,000 units in 2006. Regarding how challenging the Chinese environment was regarding market penetration, finally entry modes were devised that included three theory streams:

(1) An entry mode theory for profit maximization under a tariff model;
(2) A network theory to explain the mechanisms of global supply network adaptation; and

(3) Resource dependency theory, to understand how firms utilized available resources within the value chain network and responded to environmental uncertainties.[8]

The primary objectives accordingly were for both the original equipment manufacturer (OEM) and its suppliers to secure component sources that would save total cost requirements in their value chains. The conceptual framework—of the OEM and the suppliers' joint consideration of the details about establishing plants in other countries—needs additional emphasis. Segregating the portfolios of suppliers into three groups and grouping labor cost ratio with transportation cost ratio into high and low labor-intensive and capital-intensive groups would be an ideal process. Included are these portfolios of automobile parts suppliers: (1) low annual production, under 50,000; (2) medium annual production, from 50,000 to 120,000; and (3) high annual production, above 120,000.[9]

Conceptual Framework

There are different types of conceptual theories used to characterize SCM. The first is a resource dependency theory. The second is a supplier network theory, which develops a supplier portfolio entry model based on profit maximization under the tariff model by presenting two types of supply chain partners: those that buy and those that sell; they distinguish between the two categories. Hence, the consensus supports the facts that knowledge makes for more efficient supply chains with lower costs and active organizations with higher quality outputs that enhance consumer service. How do cross-cultural differences between global buyers and suppliers influence the value of sharing information? This question does not address the dark side, which could outweigh the benefits. Some managers thought that knowledge sharing between buyers and suppliers would create a bottleneck.

In conclusion, these three A's (agile, adapt, and align) represent the value of knowledge in global supply chains. They also point out why knowledge sharing was controversial. Of course, the greater the disparity between the market environments of buyers and suppliers, the greater the likelihood that partners will be willing to share knowledge. Supply chain partners often focus too much on their share of the benefits pie, forgetting that sharing knowledge resources benefits one another in SCM. In the competitive landscape of global chains, companies believed that sharing knowledge resulted in a competitive edge for SCM. They laid the framework and asserting that any company that had a global supply chain needed to consider introducing its strategic left hand to its operational right hand. In order words, communication is the key, and knowledge sharing becomes inevitable to the success of the partnership. Strategic supply chain planning that combines aspects of business strategy formulation with aspects of tactical supply chain planning can make each far more valuable. Combining the two scenarios may lead to competitive advantages.

A reliable source for managers who require a cost-effective technique to simulate managing disruptions in their company's supply chain is the Petri-Net (PN) framework. Petri Nets uses real-time control of supply chain networks and risk management to analyze complex systems. A graphical technique offers a mathematical foundation to analyze complex systems.[10] PN works as a tool to conduct a tabletop exercise (TTX) between the leading executives and suppliers in testing companies' capabilities to plan and respond to supply chain disruptions. It uses normal accident theory and disruptions in a supply chain to mitigate multiple perspectives. Postponement requires a delay in processing activities until precise customer order information becomes available about consumer demand.[11] The role of postponement with normal accident theory explores the complexity of measures to reduce disruptions.

A case study in the food industry illustrated how a limited Petri-Nets framework could examine a supply chain network encountering risks. A failure mode, effects, and critical analysis (FMECA) technique analyzed supply chain disruptions. Further studies showed that risk management action could improve system performance, and mitigation scenarios could reduce costs. There are also models for disruptions in supply chain management and procurement issues. Furthermore, managers should consider trade-offs between inventory policies and disruption risks in a dual sourcing supply chain network that apply to different types of interruptions. Comparison of risk-averse decision makers with neutral risk decision makers, maximizing utility or maximizing profit, respectively, is another reliable source for managers who are developing policies to respond to a company's using dual-sourcing supply chains that are at high risk for disruptions. Applying a risk management theory can safeguard against monopolistic practices that may disrupt a company's supply-chain. This study provided examples of real-world situations where supply chain disruptions occurred and replicated in a tabletop exercise (TTX) planning and responding to such disruptions.[13] This is another reliable source for managers who are considering various methods to deal with disruptions in a company's supply chain—from using normal accident theory, meaning characteristics of catastrophic accidents, to the use of postponement as a method of mitigating supply chain disruptions. The postponement approach could serve as a decision-making tool for managers participating in a tabletop exercise (TTX) to reduce supply chain disruptions.

Having no or new risk management plans for a company's supply chain can have a severe impact on a firm. A lightning fire at a sub-supplier plant in 2000 destroyed equipment used to make a radio frequency chip for Ericsson. Because the chip was sole-sourced by the supplier, production was lost, and Ericsson dropped from the mobile phone terminal business, costing $2.4 billion.[14] Based on the findings of this study, firms may improve procedures to integrate supply chain risk management into their corporate strategies. The periodic use of TTXs may validate the feasibility and effectiveness of supply-chain risk management processes.[15]

The diffusion of agility and cluster competitiveness in the oil and gas supply chains entails that agility relates to the firm and consequently its supply chain to respond and adapt to a business environment characterized by dynamic and continuous change.[16] For the firm, and hence the supply chain, agility has different meanings and definitions in the literature by various authors. Each proposes four dimensions of agility, including customer enrichment, cooperating to compete, mastering change, and uncertainty. These leverage the impact of people and information, and related attributes crucial to competition and business performance of the oil and gas industry.[17]

International Organization for Standardization

The International Organization for Standardization (ISO) is the most widely adopted private or voluntary environmental program in the world. The ISO is the most prominent global standard-setting body. It encourages firms to adopt environmental stewardship practices, not only by obeying environmental laws of the jurisdiction in which they function but also by accepting policies beyond regulatory requirements. Firms that demonstrate full compliance with standardized environmental regulations receive certificates after scrutiny by third-party auditors.[18]

The application of this tool of the partnership model seems to be a way forward for a lasting profitability between two companies. Nevertheless, the drivers behind each company's desire for the partnership will allow managers to examine the conditions that facilitate or hamper cooperation and provide a structure for measuring outcomes. The partnership model also points out the drivers and compelling reasons to partner as well as expectations of results. Furthermore, the partnership model depicts the decision to create a partnership, the components, and outcome facilitators by arguing that management components for partnerships include planning style, joint operating controls, communication, and risk/ reward sharing. The partnership model has produced a greater level of trust between two companies and resulted in a higher level of quality assurance for SCM partnership alliances.[19]

When using a strategic supply chain model, managers are trying to determine how much the opportunity cost of a particular decision differs from the model's recommendation. Additionally, a variety of industries has successfully used optimization-based tools, including one called Strategic Analysis of Integrated Logistics Systems (SAILS). For each scenario, supply chain planners can create multiple scenarios to run with their optimization models and can assert different phases those managers could use to achieve strategic supply chain planning. The steps include scenario building, scenario planning, scanning, and the business environment. Recommending the joint use of scenario planning and optimization models will be the ideal to reach shareholders' values more efficiently than using either approach in isolation.

Supply Chain Risk Management

Supply chain risk management is the decision made to reduce risk and consequences in the collective autonomous enterprises responsible for the design, procurement, manufacturing, and distribution product phases of an extended enterprise.[20] Therefore, supply chain risk management categorically stems into four parts: product complexity, regulatory requirements, resource availability, and security, embedded into a firm's sustainability strategy. There is a need to plan production in order to meet customers' demands for goods and services in both the short run and the long run. As a manager plans for internal risk factors, there are also external risk factors, which include regulatory risks. The need to make resources available to support planned activities is critical. Security has become a significant factor of production well represented in the overall enterprise budget. The decision-making trade-offs among procurement, manufacturing, logistics, and customer accommodation as determined by total costs, returns, and revenue measures equally consider risks.

Supply Chain Risk Management and Corporate Strategy

Disruptions described as major breakdowns in the production or distribution nodes that compromise a supply chain include fire, natural disasters, terrorism, and so forth. Some companies are risk-averse, whereas some are not. In spite of the corporate risk appetite, the manager considers business risks inevitable and becomes proactive to create strategies to hedge apparent liability.[21] The impact of a disruption in a supply chain can negatively affect profitability, shareholder value, distribution, and production.

The implications and consequences of disruptions in one part of the supply chain can affect the rest of the chain.[22] The effects of market interest rate volatility are overwhelming, and organizational leaders should ensure that fluctuation of exchange rates is addressed by finding the appropriate hedging strategy to handle price volatility, appropriate price contracts with suppliers, and design of robust networks. Failure to set a feasible plan for lean production concepts by itself creates problems for supply-chain risk management. Being adaptive to uncertainty in global supply chain management provides a sustained competitive advantage.[23]

Concepts and Modes Mitigating Supply Chain Disruptions

There are concepts and frameworks in literature available to managers and other organizational leaders at the strategic, tactical, and execution levels consisting of design, planning, implementation, and monitoring. Conventional accident theory uses postponement as a supply-chain risk management tool to delay the creation of utilities until customer demand is complete, allowing flexibility to react to disruption.[24] Risk management theory holds that flexibility exists in multiple sourcing to safeguard against monopolistic practices. For instance, the multivalent base framework is a computer simulation that facilitates collaborative disruption for supply chain manufacturing. PN provides a graphical technique that offers a mathematical foundation to analyze complex systems and real-time control of supply chain networks and risk management. An integrated framework should include financial hedging and operational hedging to manage exchange rate risks. This precise definition explains all of the intricate aspects of global supply-chain risk management. The managerial selection process for global supply-chain management strategies is vague. The technology implemented in the supply-chain risk management process improves over time, but the internal validity of the study may decline. These three moderators explained the process of global supply-chain risk management. A risk management theory is available for global supply chains. The risk management theory guides managers to choose a risk management strategy for global supply chains. The developed risk management theory for global supply chain management could expand to other supply chain levels. No studies explained a process for testing the combined frameworks for global supply-chain risk management.

Testing Supply Chain Risk Management Processes

Organizations can use a tabletop exercise to close the gap in testing the risk management plans that mitigate a firm's global supply chain from disruptions. A tabletop exercise (TTX) is a concept used by the militaries of several major countries in planning for combat and humanitarian assistance/disaster relief missions. The TTX includes key executive leaders, facilitators, and observers, but no products or other subordinate personnel are necessary to complete the exercise. An internal department or consulting agency monitors and provides feedback on the exercise to improve risk management processes. The TTX introduces vignettes that address most probable and worst-case scenarios that are feasible in a company's supply chain. Executives interviewed may provide insight into the construction of the disruptive nature in the vignettes.

The organization and its suppliers may improve their relationships and information-sharing capability. Managers may also identify flaws in the risk management plan and redesign the project. Facilitators could validate the computer simulation software used in risk mitigation decision-making in the supply chain. Response time to react to a disturbance in the supply chain would improve. The designated tools found in previous literature determine measures of success. The TTX is a cost-effective method for testing a plan for supply-chain risk management. Having no or new risk management plans for a company's supply chain can have a severe impact on the entire firm. Again, the lightning fire at a sub-supplier plant in the year 2000 destroyed equipment used to make a radio frequency chip for Ericsson. Because the chip was sole-sourced by the supplier, production was lost, and Ericsson dropped from the mobile phone terminal business, costing $2.4 billion.[25] Based on the findings of this study, firms may improve procedures to integrate supply chain risk management into their corporate strategies. Periodic use of TTXs validates the feasibility and effectiveness of supply-chain risk management.

Supply Chain Collaboration

Retail supply chain collaboration (SCC) contributes to the improvement of overall performance via increasing revenues, refining forecasts, improving customer service, and reducing inventory costs.[26] To be efficient and cost effective, total costs across supply chains need minimization. In today's volatile business environment, retail supply-chain collaboration plays an incredible role in transforming supply chain management. The success of many businesses lies in having effective and efficient supply chain collaboration. When two or more businesses share common management, planning, execution, and performance measurement information in partnership, it promotes greater business opportunities and enhances increased performance.

Collaboration efforts are not immune to environmental business challenges; the challenges may be external or internal. These challenges remain ubiquitous. Furthermore, the multiple pitfalls of supply-chain collaboration challenges include lack of trust, conflict of interest, cultural differences, foreign exchange transactions, and translation. Of course, the benefits outweigh the challenges. The ideal method used by most retailer supply-chains is the system dynamics simulation modeling approach. In our competitive and unpredictable business environment, changes to customer service improvements, sales volumes, and forecasting improvement are not usually attributable to happenstance. The process of disseminating information among the supply chain is vital to the success of the supply chain. In addition, knowledge management (KM) plays a significant role in information sharing among supply chain management.

Figure 4.1
Designing and creative thinking

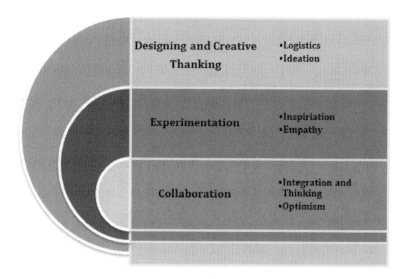

Figure 4.2
Trends in innovation

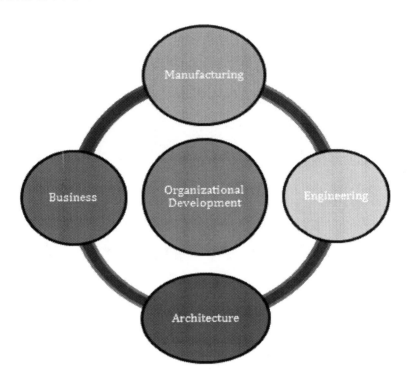

Figure 4.3
The value chain of an organization

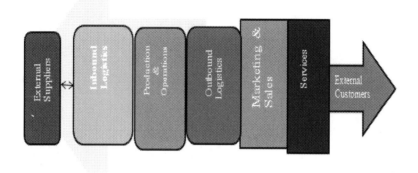

Firm Infrastructure

Human Resource Management

Technology Development

Procurement

Source: *Handbook of Global Supply Chain Management* (Mentzer, Myers, & Stank, 2007)

Figure 4.4
Model supply chain demand management

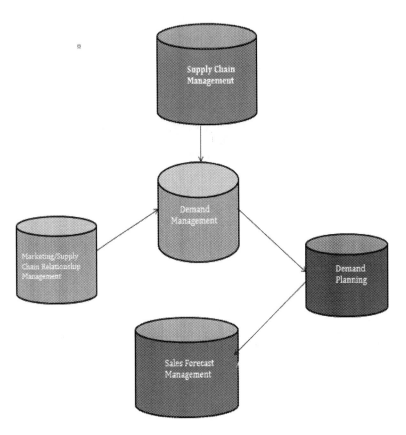

Source: *Global Supply Chain Management* (Mentzer et al., 2007)

Chapter 5

Information Technology and Innovation

Change is the law of life. And those who look only to the past or present are certain to miss the future.
—John F. Kennedy

Innovation distinguishes between a leader and a follower.
—Steve Jobs

Information technology sets the new pace to maximize profits in an organization. Innovation is the bedrock of transformational knowledge in human history. In corporate America, technology plays a predominant role in leading the global marketplace. Firms and individual countries have gained tremendously from the competitive advantage gained from information technology. Countries may become technological leaders in developing or advancing a particular technology and marketing its acquired technological advantage via licensing. The development of corn syrup as a sugar substitute decreased US dependency on sugarcane importation from South America.[1] Many companies are still receiving returns from IT investments that are below their potential. One of the risks associated with IT includes lower profits or the likelihood of obsolescence.[2] Technologies rapidly change with time. Innovation in technology, therefore, is critical to gaining competitive advantage; analytics competitors make skillful use of statistics and modeling to improve a wide variety of functions.[3]

Information Technology and Corporate America

Innovation management is the decision made to accomplish sustainable enterprises and economic reality that connect industry, society, and the environment. High-definition televisions by now should be a tremendous success globally. Companies like Philips, Sony, and Thompson invested billions of dollars in developing TV sets with high-quality pictures. From a technology perspective, they succeeded: console manufacturers have read mass market since the 1990s.[4] Conventional wisdom holds that the success of our real future rests on building sustainable enterprises and economic reality that connect, society, industry and the environment. Furthermore, much of corporate America and innovation were not very new. The waves of continuous technological change already occurred before the Industrial Age, sparking innovations including the steam engine in the eighteenth century; railroads, steel, electrification, and telecommunications in the nineteenth century; and auto and air transport, synthetic fibers, and television in the first half of the twentieth century.[5]

The challenge today is to develop a sustainable business that is compatible with the current economic reality; the best innovation business models and products may not be profitable. For a manager to depend only on ecoefficiency may distract companies from pursuing radically different products and business models. The world in which critical corporate decisions were feasible behind closed doors is disappearing. Various compelling experiences of corporate America help to illustrate this; for instance, consider the experience of Xerox in 1969. Xerox Corporation, the leading copier company, had a storied history of innovation. Some of this innovation arose from Xerox's Palo Alto Research Center (PARC), which aimed at creating a new market for the Xerox computer industry. One of the primary bottlenecks facing innovation and threatening its validity is that there are only a few Thomas Edison in today's marketplace.[6]

Organizational Learning and Knowledge Management

Knowledge management (KM) is the name of the concept in which an organization consciously and comprehensively gathers, organizes, shares, and analyzes its knowledge regarding resources, documents, and people's skills. As early as 1998, a few business enterprises had a widespread KM practice in operation.[7] In today's marketplace, with advances in technology and processing of information, many companies now impose strong knowledge management. Of course, to remain relevant and more sustainable, managers and business leaders need not delve into IT consciousness without being objective in admitting their lack of expertise in this field. KM does not involve only facts mining but also some methods of operations to push information to users.[8]

Before, implementing a KM plan, there should be a survey of complete corporate goals and a close examination of tools, both traditional and technical that will address the needs of the firm involved. The challenge of selecting a KM system to purchase or building software that fits the context of the overall project and encourages employees to use the system and share information requires careful consideration. Finally, the goal of a KM system is to provide users and others with the ability to locate and organize relevant content and the expertise required to address specific business tasks.[9] Some KM systems can analyze the relationships among materials, people, topics, and activity and produce a knowledge map report or knowledge management.

Some SME leaders fail to implement technology-based tactics to build their businesses. These organizational leaders may avoid the use of the Internet due to lack of information technology (IT) competencies. E-business allows a firm to seize market opportunities through the growth of Internet usage. For instance, with an e-business enabling innovation, corporate America can buy and sell at a lower cost than it would ordinarily. Corporate America seems to benefit more from improved IT knowledge. An understanding of IT allows companies to use necessary technology in a creative manner by increasing organizational value. Corporate leaders should plan to support the need for a fundamental IT understanding with the need to spur innovation in e-business applications. Exploring the underpinnings of competitive advantage in individual companies includes first-, second-, and third-generation knowledge management, as outlined in Figure 5.1. This includes evolutionary development, intellectual capital, organizational learning, ethical social innovation, social learning, and business innovation. The focus of this chapter on information technology and innovation includes to explore and appreciate the degree of IT competitive advantage and to discuss the positive impact of IT competitive advantage in corporate America. The chapter will also explore the background and the conceptual framework, as well as indicate particular areas of further research in this topic that would prove beneficial. What potential impact might this topic have on the overall state of competitive advantage, as well as future directions of competitive advantage research in years to come?

Competitive advantage depicts activities, decisions, and practices that elevate an idea to the realization for generating business value. Competitive advantage occurs as an organization acquires or develops an attribute that allows it to outperform its competitors. These characteristics can include access to natural resources, such as high-grade ores or nominal power, or access to highly trained and skilled workers.[11] New technology such as robotics and IT can also provide a competitive advantage as a part of the products themselves, as a benefit to the making of the products, or as a competitive aid in the business process. In today's globalized marketplace, the sustainable IT competitive advantage is pivotal for organizational performance in corporate America. The growth and profitability of this sector are incumbent on continued implementation of new ideas in information management. Most corporations fail to implement technology-based tactics to build their businesses. The information age can be vociferous and ubiquitous, revolutionizing business management and providing new ideas to maximize business growth and profitability. In our competitive marketplace, knowledge management contributes immensely to the continued growth and development of corporate America. Companies that fail to adopt and implement new technology-based tactics to build their businesses undoubtedly will continue to struggle for existence.

The inability to sense and respond to changes in the market quickly has led to the demise of many firms with household names on the East Coast of the United States, including Circuit City, Kmart, and a host of others. Therefore, it is critical that managers identify and comprehend strategic orientations that enable business performance and sustainability. An organization achieves market-based sustainability to the extent that it strategically aligns itself with market-oriented products, needs, and wants of customers and the interest of multiple stakeholders.[12] Of course, nothing supersedes a business providing value and meeting the needs of its clients at low costs.

Information Systems

An information system is an elaborate set of components for gathering, processing, and storing data and for delivering information, knowledge, and digital products.[13] The Information Age has revolutionized our everyday life for good. The information system is more prevalent in today's World Wide Web (WWW) than the Internet. As you already know, the Internet is a collection or conglomeration of a network of computers connecting millions of people globally. Before I delve into the practical details of information systems, I would like to lay the foundation of the following web terms: website, website address, the (uniform resource locator), web browser, search engines, blog, and social networking sites.

Website. Website relates to a particular site on the web that you can visit.

Website address. The website address is a particular name that signifies and identifies a unique site on the web, for example, www. baseball.com.

URL. As the name suggests, the uniform resource locator is a unique web page within a particular website.

Web browser. The term web browser applies to software that enables one to surf the Internet, for example, Internet Explorer, Firefox, and Google Chrome.

Search engines. As the name implies, a search engine is a tool on the web to assist the user in finding a site for information or service.

Blog. A blog is similar to a journal on a website.

Social networking sites. As the name implies, a social networking site is a particular site used to post personal information about oneself, create a network of friends, and share contents such as photographs and the like. Social networking should remain private and not formal. The popular ones today include MySpace with more than 200 million users and Facebook, to mention only a couple.

Management Information Systems

Every level of management uses a computerized database of financial information organized to generate reports on operations. A management information system (MIS) helps to facilitate the process by creating various types of special reports easily. Organizational leaders and managers need MIS to receive feedback about their operating performances. Additionally, MIS is ideal for analyzing and comparing information within the organization as a whole. Information displayed by the MIS typically shows actual data over planned results and outcomes from a year before; thus, it measures progress against goals.[14] The MIS enables managers to routinely receive programmable reports that are run at intervals or on demand, while others are obtained using built-in query languages; supervisors can check on status at desk-side computers connected to the MIS by networks that use display functions built into the system. Many sophisticated systems also monitor and display the company's stock performance on a periodic basis. Management information systems (MIS) are a significant business function and a conduit that propels our information digital age.

Business intelligence

In corporate America, organizations need more than just information and data. Organizations need collections of customers, competitors, and internal operations of the organization. Business intelligence enables corporate America to extract the real meaning of information to make strategic decisions to ensure competitive advantage in the marketplace. There are four primary IT tools used for business intelligence (BI):

(a) Database,
(b) Database management,
(c) Data mining, and
(d) Data warehouse.

Additionally, there are two distinct terms useful in processing and understanding BI, namely, online analytical processing (OLAP) and online transaction processing (OLTP).

Online Analytical Processing. OLAP is the use of information to support decision-making within an organization. In most businesses, OLAP is inevitable. The creation of a data warehouse relates to organizing and using stored information to support decision-making in an organization regarding its vast array of selling strategies and marketing campaign information.

Data Warehousing. A data warehouse is a typical form of information gathered from an operational database for supporting decision-making schemes. When an organization builds a data warehouse and uses data mining tools such as OLTP and OLAP to manipulate the data warehouse's information, the goal is to create business intelligence. BI supports managers' harnessing of data to enhance decision-making.

As you can see in figure 5.3, you can query the operational database to collect basic kinds of BI, such as how many products or items of inventory an employee sold in a month or a quarter over $5,000, and how much money the organization spent on marketing. Whereas the results of such a query may be significant and helpful, you still need to combine the numbers and kinds of products sold as well as the marketing information with other types of information within the organization, including customer names and other demographics, to perform online analytical processing. Furthermore, you can perform detailed queries to garner BI from a data warehouse, more than you could collect from one database. For instance, what new marketing strategies do you need to reach customers with a required increased level of income to meet targeted sales figures?

Online Transaction Processing. Online transaction processing relates to the process of gathering, processing, and updating existing information to reflect the gathered input information. As you can see in figure 5.4, I have created a view of a portion of a wholesale retailer's database. These tables contain five separate files: order, customer, product type, employee, and product number. There are specific relationships among these data. The customer places an order; employees sell the products, and so on. To manage the customer relationship and process the orders, you need all these files and much more. Each of the files contains attributes: for instance, the order file contains order date, customer name, number, and product number. The customer file contains customer number, product number, customer's name, employee ID number, and date of hire. These are all significant pieces of information for the organization to process efficiently and manage customer order relationships.

Database Management Systems and Data Warehousing

Databases and data warehousing are IT tools organizations use to manage and store valuable customer information. The database contains large repositories of extensive information in every organization. Management is duly responsible for the safety and security of this vital information. For example, when you buy a product from an American store, the details of the sales transaction, such as the credit card number used, your name, and the items purchased, are very significant information to the business organization. Such information becomes an essential commodity to the company. This personal information has become an increasing problem of identity theft in corporate America. Perhaps if you are not yet a victim, one of your friends or someone else you know must have in one way or another experienced identity theft. The Bank of America had 1.2 million of its customers' identities stolen. TJX Companies reported a more stunning information loss from 2005 to 2007: 45.6 million.[15] The database is the technique used to store this information. A data warehouse is a special form of database that consists of information gathered from an operational database to support decision-making within an organization.

Rational database. The rational database model is an IT tool used to organize and access information according to its logical structure, not according to its physical position. In other words, you do not care in which row the item or information appears. You only need to understand the employee ID number and the product identification number. The data dictionary contains the logical structure in a database model. For example, the data dictionary for Customer Order will contain nine digits. The data dictionary for Date of Hire in the employee file requires day, month, and year. This type of organizational information is unique from the usual process of row number and column characters. Processing a rational database requires one to know only the name of the field and the column of information and its logical row. One may define a relational database as two-dimensional tables used to organize and store information, as shown in figure 5.5. It includes (a) the information itself, stored in two-dimensional tables or files, and (b) the logical structure of that information.[16]

Data mining. As the name suggests, data mining is the process of designing, configuring, an organization's anomalies, and finding correlations within multiple data sets to predict outcomes.[17] This valuable IT tool uses a multiplicity of techniques. Corporate America may use this information to project total revenues, reduce costs, reduce risks, and improve customer relationships. If you were born in the late 1990s, you might have missed learning and using other types of office equipment unlike personal computers in processing information. Before the era of personal computers and the Internet, the type of equipment used in processing information included data processing, typewriters, and floppy disks. Advances in today's processing power and speed have galvanized us to go beyond the manual, time-consuming techniques to a quick and automated data analysis.[18] Data mining is the tool used by governments and business organizations such as banks, insurance companies, retailers, manufacturers, telecommunication providers, and a host of others to process and discover relationships among more complex data sets collected.

Figure 5.1
Innovation management

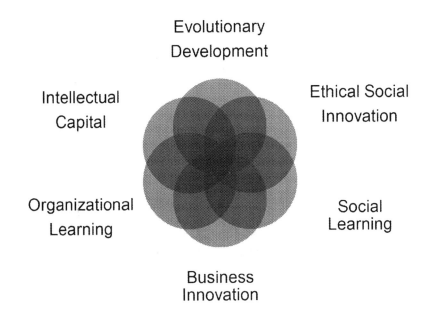

Figure 5.2
Strategic management and corporate America

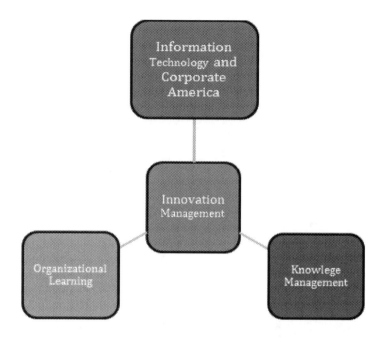

Figure 5.3
Business intelligence structure

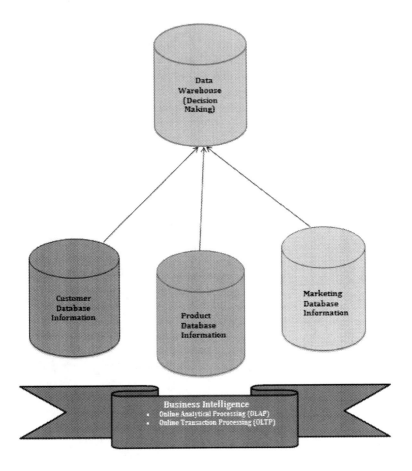

Figure 5.4
Database for customer relationship management

Order Date	Company Name	Customer Order #	Quality	Price	Product ID
09/05/2015	Dell	123456789	100	$75	012345
09/11/2015	HP	222222333	120	$155	022333
09/15/2015	IBM	098765432	150	$350	033444
10/01/2015	Phillips	111222333	280	$200	044555
10/10/2015	Gateway	222333666	30	$650	055666

Customer Sales File

Purchase Order Number	Company Name	Item Description	Product Type	Qty.	Price	Product ID
P.O.Z0021	Best Buy	Laptop	1	50	320	012345
P.O.B0021	Wal-Mart	Desktop	2	100	235	022333
P.O.D0021	Big K-Mart	Desktop	3	120	235	033444
P.O.S0021	BJ Store	Laptop	4	180	155	044555
P.O.T0021	Cisco	Desktop	5	200	189	055666

Employee File

Employee ID	Employee Last Name	Employee First Name	Product ID	Date of Hire
055555555	James	Johnson	012345	2/1/1988
066666666	Matthew	Jude	022333	5/5/1990
077777777	Jones	Mark	033444	8/10/1965
088888888	Dadson	Judy	044555	10/09/1978
099999999	Clark	Edward	055666	9/4/1968

Figure 5.5
Logical ties with prime and critical keys

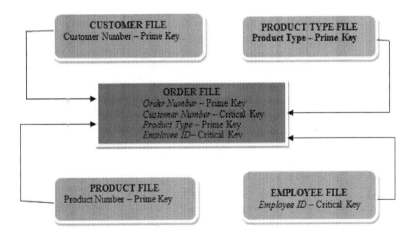

Source: *Management Information Systems (Haag & Cummings, 2008)*

Chapter 6

Strategic Business Management

In matters of style, swim with the current; in matters of principle,
stand like a rock.
—Thomas Jefferson

The heart and soul of a company is creativity and innovation.
—Frederick W. Smith, CEO of FedEx

Every day organizational leaders face operational and strategic challenges requiring top-management decision-making. Strategic management involves the formulation and implementation of the major goals and initiatives taken by a company's top management on behalf of stockholders or owners based on available resources. Operational management is concerned primarily with improving efficiency and controlling costs within the boundaries set by the organization's strategy. Therefore, strategic management is about the strategies that organizational leaders use to achieve better performance. Strategic business management encompasses the assessment of external and internal environs of the organization to gain competitive advantage.[1] Strategic business management provides overall direction for the organization, specifying the organization's primary objectives and developing plans and policies to achieve the set goals.

Business Management

Business management is the key function in management that coordinates the efforts of people to accomplish goals and objectives by using available resources to minimize cost and increase output, productivity, and profitability. Business management also involves organizational leaders setting different goals for the accomplishment of various purposes within an organization. An organization is like our human anatomy; it has different interchangeable parts with separate functions. Business management is the key instrument to ignite the various intertwining parts to achieve a common organizational goal.

There are seventeen essential elements of internal control to ensure better functionality of every business organization in corporate America. Figure 6.1 depicts the new Committee of Sponsoring Organizations (COSO) of the Treadway Commission framework that management may find helpful in implementing internal controls. The COSO recently released its updated internal control framework to provide more comprehensive and relevant practical guidance focusing on assisting management to concentrate on the significant areas of the component of internal control. The COSO ERM (Enterprise Resource Management) model focuses on the following components: why, what, and where. The model succinctly supplements the original five COSO elements: control environment, control activities, risk assessment, monitoring, and information and communication.

Control environment. As the name suggests, the control environment is the tone at the top, as sometimes called. This is the highest level of management that makes the most significant organizational decisions in any organization. The control environment sets the policies and procedures of the organization.

Control activities. Control activity is the second level in the management hierarchy. This is the level of managers responsible for the enforcement of the policies and procedures envisaged by the top management level. It includes the CEO and the CFO of the organization. Organizations may arrange control activity vertically or horizontally (e.g., line managers).

Risk assessment. Risk assessment is another critical element of management control within an organization. Risks are mostly inevitable for organizations in today's volatile business environment. Some organizations may be risk averse, whereas the majority is not. Risk assessment is the significant element of controls that assesses the various risks that are inherent to business organizations.

Monitoring. As the name implies, monitoring is one of the controls' features to ensure the daily activities of the organization regarding set goals, policies, and procedures implemented about set standards Monitoring handles providing all the necessary feedbacks to top management concerns on daily operational activities of the business organization. Therefore, monitoring is a significant element of every organization.

Information and communication. Information and knowledge are more useful within an organization when they are not restricted from communicating and sharing. The dissemination of information is critical in every management. The management of every organization needs current and meaningful information to operate efficiently. Today's business environment requires instant and current information to make significant business decisions, and management depends immensely on the information and communication control elements to provide appropriate feedback.

Enterprise Resource Management (ERM)

After the high-profile business scandals and failures in the early 2000s, corporate America created a model in 2004 that expanded a broader understanding of the entity's overall strategies and goals, and the threats to those plans and objectives.[3] The resulting ERM model expands upon, rather than replaces, the earlier integrated framework for internal control in business management. Similar to other integrated framework models, the ERM model framework augments, rather than changes, the process.

Corporate America has come to terms with the fact that the path to sustainable growth and profitability in today's rapidly changing business environment includes managing innovation and IT competitive advantage effectively. Effective IT competition has become an essential requirement for staying competitive in today's marketplace. In fact, the primary determinants of achieving long-term sustainability in corporate America emanate from the firm's ability to competently direct innovation resources to address the new emerging markets and economic environment.[5]

Competition in the marketplace defines an organizational strategy. Thus, organizational structure is the driving force behind operations and the foundation upon which both short-term and long-term decisions come to fruition. Most organizations have some strategies in place at any given time: a marketing strategy, a personnel strategy, and operations strategies. All of these strategies derive from the overall organizational strategy and mission statement. Competitive-Intensity-Numerous (CIN) models have been developed to help formulate corporate strategies.[6] The widely used model developed by Michael Porter and known as Porter's Five Forces, as depicted in figure 6.2, evaluates the competitive intensity of the organization's industry by analyzing the market in five dimensions.[7]

Porter's Five Competition Forces

According to Porter, the five forces that shape industry competition are (a) the threat of new entrants, (b) the threat of substitute products or services, (c) rivalry among existing competitors, (d) bargaining power of buyers, and (e) bargaining power of suppliers.

The threat of new entrants. Factors that influence the ability of new companies to enter the market include

(a) The amount of capital required to enter the market,
(b) The extent of government regulation of the industry,
(c) The existence of brand identity and loyalty,
(d) The existence of product patents,
(e) The availability of distribution channels, and
(f) The existence of other barriers to entry, and the easier it is for companies to enter the market, the more the potential for competition within the market.[8]

The threat of new entrants is a major factor in a competitive market. Therefore, organizational leaders need to pay particular attention to ensuring the availability of adequate resources and efforts.

The threat of substitute products. The availability of alternative products or technologies limits the competitive strategies available to the organization. Furthermore, low levels of perceived product differentiation, low costs to switch from one product to another, little difference in performance between alternative products, and low costs of substitute products significantly aggravate the threat of a substitute product to the organization. Other factors may potentially lead to threats of substitute products or services. These factors include buyer propensity to substitute products or services, the availability of a close substitute, ease of substitution, perceived level of product differentiation, and buyer switching costs or taste. For example, Coke and Pepsi are close substitute products.

Rivalry among existing competitors. In most industries, the intensity of competitive rivalries is a primary determinant of competitiveness in the industry. Porter's five forces framework recognizes some potential factors that may lead to competitive rivalry, including the degree of transparency, sustainable competitive advantage via innovation, a firm's concentration ratio, the level of advertising expense, and a powerful competitive strategy. Most strategy consultants use Porter's five forces framework when evaluating a firm's strategic position and not for line-of-business industry level. The current level of competition in the market also limits the competitive strategies available to the organization. The factors to consider when evaluating current competition are

(a) The number and diversity of competitors in the market,
(b) The existence of barriers to exit, and
(c) The growth rate of the market.

The presence of a vast number of competitors, high barriers to exiting, and/or a low growth rate make it much harder for an organization to compete.[9] Analysis of the five forces provides an understanding of the marketplace's competitive forces, upon which the organization's competitive strategy emerges. This analysis shows how a firm can use these forces to obtain a sustainable competitive advantage. Porter modifies Chandler's dictum about structure by introducing a second level of structure: organizational structure follows strategy, which in turn follows industry setting. Porter's generic strategies detail the interaction between cost minimization strategies, product differentiation strategies, and market focus strategies.[10]

Bargaining power of buyers. In an analysis of customer characteristics and the choices in product options available to them, features of interest include

(a) Size of the customer base,
(b) Buyer volume,
(c) Availability of substitute products, and
(d) Cost of switching to alternate products.

In general, environments in which there are relatively few customers, where alternative products are available, where the cost of switching to alternative products is small, and/or where high-volume purchases are common tend to favor the customer and create a more challenging competitive environment. The bargaining power of the buyer is fundamental to the factors influencing competition.

Bargaining power of suppliers. In an analysis of provider characteristics that affect the ability of the organization to negotiate for favorable treatment when purchasing materials or services, features of interest include

(a) Number of suppliers and the number of available firms,
(b) Availability of alternative products, and
(c) The cost of switching to an alternate product input.

When there are relatively few suppliers, few alternative products, and/or when the cost of switching to an alternative product is high, the supplier has an advantage over the buyer; the buyer's inability to negotiate effectively limits the competitive options available to him or her.

Determinants of Generic Competitive Strategies

There are two primary generic competitive strategies: the product or service differentiation strategy and the cost leadership strategy. An organization's competitive strategy defines the way in which it positions itself to compete in the marketplace. Porter's model identifies two generic strategies of competition in broad, typically national or international, markets: product differentiation and cost leadership.

Product differentiation. A differentiated product perceived to offer unique features or benefits to the customer (e.g., gasoline that contains additives to improve engine longevity) inspires higher levels of brand loyalty in customers, making them less sensitive to price differences among products. To compete using the strategy of product differentiation, an organization must foster continued product innovation and improvement through investment in research and development, as well as effectively market the product to maintain the brand distinction. Caterpillar Corporation and Toyota Corporation of America use the product differentiation strategy in gaining competitive advantage in their industries.

Cost leadership. Under this approach, first an entity will seek to be the low-cost provider in an industry for a given level of output. Secondly, an entity will sell its product or service either at the industry average price and earn a profit higher than that of other competitors in the industry or below the industry average rate so as to gain market share.[11] Thirdly, entities acquire or maintain cost advantages by

(a) Identifying and avoiding unnecessary costs,
(b) Improving process efficiency,
(c) Gaining exclusive access to lower cost inputs,
(d) Using outsourcing in an optimal manner, and
(e) Pursuing vertical integration—moving up or down in the supply chain.[12]

Cost leadership focuses on the organization's ability to sell a high volume of low-cost products. To be able to implement this strategy, organizations should have high levels of productivity and efficiency, as well as access to extensive distribution resources. Major factors affecting the successful implementation of the cost leadership strategy include (a) proprietary production technology, (b) access to low-cost production inputs (raw materials, labor, and so forth), and (c) access to low-cost capital.

It is also possible to segment the market, selecting a few target markets in which to compete rather than trying to compete in the entire market.[13] Segmentation of the marketplace yields a third competitive strategy, known as a focus strategy or, more generically, niche marketing. Segments (or niches) are based on geographic regions, population demographics, or a variety of individual interests or needs. Organizations may gain a competitive advantage by customizing the product to meet the needs of the specialized market segment. Competition within market segments can be based either on low cost (cost focus) or product differentiation (focused differentiation).[14]

Characteristics of Cost Leadership Firms

Companies that successfully carry out the cost leadership strategy typically have the following kinds of strengths: (a) significant capital to invest in production assets to keep cost low, and (b) high levels of expertise in manufacturing processes.[15] Michael Porter's five forces framework for accessing the nature, operating attractiveness, and likely long-run profitability of a competitive industry was used for this analysis. That framework includes establishing measurable goals built on the entity's strengths to take advantage of identified opportunities and to build up any weaknesses and ward off threats.

Goal setting is the process of deciding what the entity wants to accomplish.[16] The goals formulated should be (a) specific, (b) measurable, (c) attainable, (d) relevant, and (e) time-bound. The five competitive forces shape strategy. The job of a strategist is to understand competition. More often than not, managers narrowly define competition as if it only occurs among today's direct competitors. Innovation management includes a set of tools that allow organizational leaders and engineers to cooperate with a shared understanding of goals and processes.[17]

The focus of innovation management is to enable the organization to respond to external or internal opportunities and use its creative efforts to introduce new ideas, processes, or products. Significantly, competitive advantage should involve workers at every level in contributing creatively to an organization's development, manufacturing, and marketing.[18] Don't forget the five competitive forces that shape strategy: (a) threat of new entrants, (b) threat of substitute products, (c) rivalry among existing competitors, (d) bargaining power of buyers, and (e) bargaining power of suppliers.

By utilizing appropriate innovative management tools, management triggers and deploys the creative ingenuity of the whole workforce toward the development of the organization. Again, this process is an evolutionary integration of the organization, technology, and market by integrating a series of activities: search, select, capture, and implement. A sustainable IT competitive advantage helps firms to harness their competencies and gain competitive advantage. The understanding of information technology (IT) enables SMEs to use basic technology in a proactive manner to create value for their stakeholders and spur innovation. As business transforms to be knowledge-based, innovation management also ensues.

Competing in overcrowded industries was no way to sustain high performance; the real opportunity was to create a business of uncontested market space. Corporate America created demand rather than fought over limited opportunities, and that was many opportunities for growth that was both profitable and rapid.[19] Those firms that accepted taking advantage of these new ideas and reversed their business models succeeded against the odds. Corporate America has come to terms with the idea that the path to sustainable growth and profitability in today's volatile business environment includes managing innovation and IT competitive advantage effectively. Lastly, effective IT competition has become an essential requirement for staying competitive in today's market. In fact, the primary determinants of achieving long-term sustainability in organizations emanate from the firms' ability to competently direct innovation resources to address the evolving market and economic environment.

Competitive advantage indicates activities, decisions, and practices that elevate an idea to realization for generating business value. Competitive advantage occurs as an organization acquires or develops attributes that allow it to outperform its competition. These characteristics can include access to natural resources, such as high-grade ores or nominal power, or access to highly trained and skilled workers.[20] New technology such as robotics and IT can also provide a competitive advantage, as a part of the product itself, as a benefit to the making of the product, or as a competitive aid in the business process. In today's information age, the sustainable IT competitive advantage is pivotal for the corporate performance of organizations. The growth and profitability of an organization are incumbent on continued implementation of new ideas in information management. In today's competitive marketplace, knowledge management has contributed immensely to the continued growth and development of corporate America; companies that fail to adopt and implement new technology-based tactics to build their businesses will cease to be relevant.

Innovation and Competitiveness

The preponderance of technology and innovation in today's marketplace has not only transformed business management but also given it a face-lift. As the technological era further and further replaces the industrial age, corporate America rewards managers more for innovative ideas to encourage organizational learning and improve organizational performance. The essence of the business model was to define the manner by which the enterprise delivers value to customers, entices customers to pay for value, and converts those payments to profit.[21] In other words, for any business to remain relevant in today's competitive markets; the organizational leaders need to establish a competitive advantage to move the enterprise forward.

Hence, competitiveness is not only a business concept; it is the threshold used to determine the success or failure of most companies. It also identifies leaders and followers in the industry.[22] To be successful in today's global business environment, organizational leaders need to apply the best business practices and concepts to compete globally as well as increase business growth and development. The innovative capacities of business organizations can benefit from R&D cooperation to expand access to external knowledge. R&D cooperation among different-size firms provides more knowledge spillover for SMEs than the larger firms, thereby stimulating interest in collaboration despite constraints from management expertise and extensive intellectual property protection. Organizations that are fearful of sharing innovation secrets and therefore lean toward R&D cooperation with research institutions and universities will lose the competitive ability to absorb and exploit knowledge spillover from cooperation; such knowledge spillover is essential for small firms to be able to innovate. A quantitative examination of a nationwide innovation survey provided data to confirm a positive correlation between innovation and a company's decision to pursue R&D cooperation.

The Auto Industry

The recent challenges of the Toyota Corporation of America synchronize with the concept of business strategic management and its influence on corporate America. Toyota uses both differentiation and low cost as generic strategies to try to gain a competitive advantage over its competitors in the automotive industry. The market scope that Toyota uses is a broad one that encompasses nearly every type of customer that is in the market to purchase an automobile. Toyota can target such a large market because it has something for everyone. Toyota has four-wheel-drive trucks and SUVs for outdoor types or those who live in areas that face severe weather conditions and hybrid models like the Prius for eco-friendly customers that are interested in saving the environment, along with standard cars for general, everyday use. Additionally, Toyota provides vehicles for all price ranges. From the low-price Toyota Corolla line of cars to the high-price luxury line of cars and SUVs with Lexus, Toyota has something for people at all economic levels.

Toyota differentiates on several levels from its competitors. First, Toyota has been very successful in differentiating by superior design and quality. This has led to Toyota being able to create a brand image that is very strong and one that brings to mind quality, long-lasting cars. The strength of Toyota's brand image faced challenges in recent years with product recalls. General Motors also suffered sustained losses due to product recalls in 2015. Toyota was able to survive the recall dilemma because it had such a long and proven record of accomplishment of quality and superiority. Another area where Toyota differentiates is in technology. Toyota was the first that successfully mass-produce a hybrid car on the market; it released the Prius in 2003. Being the first to get a hybrid on the market allowed Toyota to gain a significant portion of the market share in the area of hybrid cars.

Along with differentiation, Toyota uses low cost to try to gain a competitive advantage in the automotive industry. Toyota is the low-cost producer in the industry. Toyota achieves its cost leadership strategy by adopting lean production, careful choice, and control of suppliers, efficient distribution, and low servicing costs for a quality product. Toyota's current grand strategies are product development and offensive strategy for industry leaders. Product development is vital for Toyota because it must come out with fresh new ideas every year in the automotive industry. In that industry, if you do not develop a new design of your products, you will begin to take a backseat or left behind very quickly. Toyota is an industry leader and has much power because of this. Toyota remains on the offensive to maintain its market share and defend against others in the industry taking its market share. Toyota always remains on the offensive looking for ways to be better than its competitors look. Toyota wants to remain in front of its competitors and take advantage of any weaknesses they may show and capitalize on them to gain any advantage it can.

As previously mentioned, Toyota is the low-cost leader in its industry. Recent events have suggested that Toyota has focused too much on low cost, losing market share and market positioning due to superior design and quality, which historically they have used as a differentiation strategy. The most important thing Toyota needs to do is to ensure that its low-cost strategy does not compromise its superior design and quality. In terms of Toyota's grand strategy, it has been successful at product development. By 2012, Toyota planned to have more than twenty models that used batteries to extend fuel economy just as the Prius did.[23] Of course; the company will continue its global market dominance. It has not been as aggressive in the electric car market lately as its competitors have been; Toyota planned to release a rechargeable version of their Prius by June 2012.[24] This rechargeable version would position Toyota to attempt to take over as a low-cost leader in hybrid technologies within the market, which supports Toyota's overall strategy of low cost.

Regarding changes in government policies and the competitiveness of the industry, Toyota took an offensive strategy. With a series of damaging safety recalls, Toyota had to reevaluate its previous track record of superior design, which caused it to temporarily lose track of its former offensive strategy of quality.[25] In the United States, Toyota will have to work extremely hard to get back to its offensive strategy and back to being the industry leader. With continued safety recalls, Toyota will continue to sustain a considerable market loss in its product. It needs to get back on track and refocused and make sure that it concentrates on what made it unique. To ensure continuity, organizational leaders of Toyota are going to have to focus on company communication and bringing back its former foundation of building quality cars that are dependable and reliable.

The company found its weak spot when it came to the way it responded to the recalls in the United States. At the beginning of the recall era, Toyota was very slow in its response. Finally, Toyota executives made the decision to recall more than 5 million of its vehicles due to numerous different issues.[26] At the same time, it decided to halt all sales of Toyota vehicles until the company addressed the problem. For a car company, this was a huge deal and one that would affect the balance sheets for years to come. Toyota was slow in finding a solution to its largest problem in the company's history—and in the industry's history. With a massive recall and halt in sales, one would assume that management would be pushing for day and night research, product development, and problem solving to get their product back on the market. Instead, it took Toyota a little over a week. The poor communication within the company would show when dealers had no idea or word from the company as to what the game plans were, especially when the United States called in several Toyota executives to congressional hearings, where finger-pointing began.[27]

The Toyota product development system uses lean manufacturing. Its objective is to integrate people, process, and technology. Toyota's product development procedure is essentially different from a manufacturing process. Its backbone is not visible, and knowledge and information about the process are restricted. The product development's cycle time is much longer than hours. It usually takes weeks or even months. The production chains are nonlinear and multidirectional. Workers are no longer manufacturing workers but specialists with diverse high technological knowledge. This product development strategy is viable for Toyota because it helps Toyota to prolong the life cycle of the current product. For instance, Toyota's Camry is a very successful model product of the company. Toyota started producing Camry in the 1980s as a mid- to high-level family vehicle. After thirty years of development, Camry is still very famous all over the world. This demonstrates Toyota's successful product development strategy. The development system personnel are functional engineering managers. They are primarily teachers in the Toyota system, which hires the most technically competent engineers, with the highest levels of experience. Toyota's management group consists of top experts. They were all engineers, and their technical excellence is famous.

However, recently, Toyota's product development system has not worked very well. In recent years, more and more recall issues have happened, and that hurt Toyota's reputation very much. Most of these recalls related to Toyota's technical problems. The gas pedal was one of the major aspects that led to many serious car accidents. This hurt Toyota's reputation and brand name very much. Through its product development strategy, Toyota was supposed to improve its product quality and technology, as well as make sure their products were safe.

The Prius is sold in over 90 markets, with Japan and the United States being its largest markets.[28] Global cumulative Prius liftback sales reached the milestone 1 million vehicle mark in May 2008, 2 million in September 2010, and passed the 3 million mark in June 2013.[29] Cumulative sales of 1 million Priuses were achieved in the US by early April 2011, and Japan reached the 1 million mark in August 2011. As of April 2016, the Prius liftback is the world's top selling hybrid car with 3.73 million units sold.[30] In 2011, Toyota expanded the Prius family to include the Prius v, an extended hatchback wagon, and the Prius c, a subcompact hatchback. In 2012, Toyota released the production version of the Prius plug-in hybrid. The second generation of the plug-in variant, the Prius Prime, is schedule for release by the end of 2016. Toyota expects the Prime to achieve the highest miles per gallon equivalent (MPGe) rating in all-electric mode of any plug-in hybrid available in the market.[31] Global sales of the Prius c variant passed the 1 million mark during the first half of 2015. The Prius family totaled global cumulative sales of 5.7 million units in April 2016, representing 63% of the 9 million hybrids sold worldwide by Toyota since 1997.[32] As of April 2016; sales of the Prius liftback in both Japan and the US had exceeded 1.6 million units.

As of April 2016, Toyota Company had sold the Prius in over 90 countries and regions. Worldwide cumulative sales of the Prius passed the 1 million mark in May 2008, exceeded 2 million units in September 2010, and reached the 3 million milestones in June 2013. As of April 2016, global sales of the Prius family totaled almost 5.7 million units representing 63% of the 9 million hybrids delivered by Toyota Motor Company (TMC) worldwide, including the Lexus brand. Sales of the Prius family stem from the Prius liftback with 3.73 million units, followed by the Aqua/Prius c with 1.25 million, the Prius +/v/α with, 634 thousand and the Prius Plug-in Hybrid with 75.4 thousand units.

Strategic Management

Figure 6.3 illustrates the strengths, weaknesses, opportunities, and threats (SWOT) analysis matrix. SWOT is a structured planning method used to evaluate the strengths, weaknesses, opportunities, and threats of a particular project or business venture. Corporate America uses SWOT analysis for products, projects, places, and industries, or on an individual basis.

Strengths. Every business decision or project has the characteristic of benefits or advantages for others.

Weaknesses. There is also the inherent possibility of business decisions placing a project at a disadvantage when compared to other alternatives.

Opportunities. Opportunities relate to the characteristics a business decision or plan may have to exploit the project's merits.

Threats. Threats are the environmental elements that can mitigate the company's judgment or projects.

Figure 6.1
The COSO ERM model

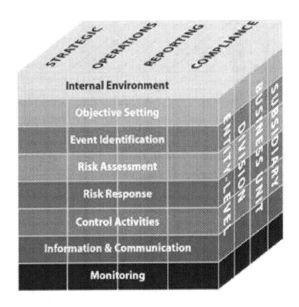

Source: Vibato: www.coso2013 solution.com

Figure 6.2
The SWOT analysis

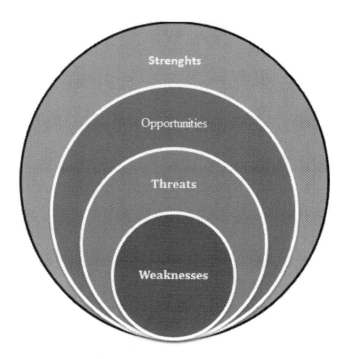

Figure 6.3
Porter's five forces, the five forces that shape industry competition

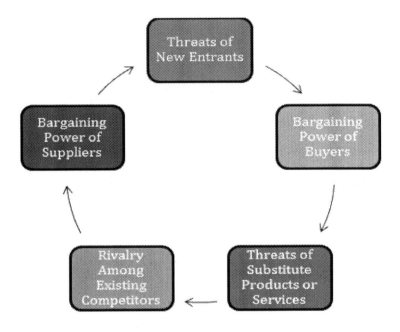

Chapter 7

Dynamism of Corporate America

You have to be very nimble and very open-minded. Your success is going to be very dependent on how you adapt.
—Larry Page, CEO of Google

The Dynamics of Corporate America and Innovation explores the nature of corporate America and innovation. It provides a concise and comprehensive review of business ownerships, emphasizes strategies to sustain business operations, describes the place of technology in business, evaluates innovation management in corporate America, and evaluates the significance of the global supply chain. The conceptual frameworks supporting this book include stakeholder theory and general systems theory.

One of the most gratifying outcomes of the research reported in this book is the finding that a business resembles a complex system, a dynamic living organism, creating wealth and value by maximizing stakeholders' profit. This discovery is gratifying because the characteristics prevalent in the dynamics of corporate America are in its profit maximization. By the traditional standards, every business, whether small or large, exists to profit; therefore, profitability becomes an acceptable threshold or a yardstick to differentiate a successful business from one that is unsuccessful.

In this book, we have learned that in their quest and search for profitability, some organizational leaders in some extraordinarily successful organizations, using the best managerial practices and techniques, have led their companies toward failure. Of course, businesses are not immune to failure. Companies must not abrogate the organizational structures, decision-making, and capabilities processes that have helped them thrive and become successful in their industries just because they sometimes failed to work due to disruptive technological change. Some of the innovation challenges faced by today's managers are sustaining. Most managers and innovators perceive failure distinctively. To the innovator, failure breeds success; but managers abhor failure because of its fiduciary obligations to its stakeholders.

In this book, we also learned that *corporate social responsibility* (CSR) is a term used in business to refer to the attitude of organizations' responses in dealing with their economic, social, and environmental impacts. CSR continues to dominate social and economic discussions. A corporation policy on CSR functions as a self-regulatory mechanism whereby the company monitors and answers its active compliance with ethical standards, the law, and national and global norms.[1] CSR aids an organization's mission as well as serves as a guide to what the company represents for its consumers. The term CSR became more popular in the 1960s and has remained used by many organizations to cover legal and moral responsibility more narrowly construed.[2] What is corporate social responsibility?

- Most large companies now incorporate social good into their brands.
- CSR is a valuable and viable practice.
- One primary focus of CSR is the environment.
- Businesses both large and small have a chunk of carbon residue.
- Any steps to reduce those residues are good for both the business and society.

A corporate ladder is a conceptualized view of an organization's employment hierarchy, in which job advancement is incumbent on climbing steps of a ladder, with entry-level positions on the bottom and executive-level positions at the top. *Climbing the corporate ladder* is a phrase used to describe one's advancement within a company through promotions.[3] Climbing the corporate ladder depends on the individual's skills and competitiveness. If an employee can demonstrate the skill and ability to give measurable value to the corporation's goals and objectives—maximizing profit—the corporate ladder becomes accessible and attainable.[4]

Theoretically, a business model constitutes an abstract representation of an organization, including its purpose, strategies, business process, offerings, target customers, infrastructure, organizational structures, sourcing, trading practices, operational processes, and culture; it also includes its policies. The business model represents the graphical, conceptual, and textual of all cores interrelated cooporational, architecturally, and in other ways, developed and designed by an organization.[5] A business model defines the rationale of how a company creates, captures, and delivers value. George and Bock (2012) defined a business model as the design of organizational structures to enact a commercial opportunity in a systematic review and analysis.[6] Further, a business model describes and classifies businesses, mostly in entrepreneurial settings; also, organizational leaders use a business model to explore future developments and possibilities in a company.

A business dictionary defines innovation as the process of translating an idea or invention into a service or goods that create value or for which consumers will pay.[7] New ideas are not innovation unless they meet the following criteria: they are (a) replicable, (b) satisfy specific needs, and (c) involve the deliberate application of information. Maryville (1992) asserted that innovation viewed as the application of better solutions that meet new requirements, unarticulated needs, or existing market needs. However, a clear distinction is necessary between invention and innovation. Bhasin (2012) argued that innovation resembles but not related to the invention. Often, a novel device appears to resemble innovation in economics, management science, and other fields of practice and analysis; but innovation results in a process that brings together various novel ideas in the way that they affect society. Innovation is not only a pivot upon which the wheels of business management thrive. Innovation also promotes creativity in an organization. If a business stops innovating, it stops being relevant. There are different types of innovation. Innovation is the result of an interactive process of knowledge mining, application, and diffusion. The significance of knowledge interactions for innovation continues to challenge today's managers and other organizational leaders.

Global supply-chain management (SCM) is a process of managing supply-chain globally and/or nationally to gain competitive advantage. A supply chain is the business concept used to form alliances or partnership relationships laterally or horizontally between one business and another to profit. Supply chain management is one of the fastest and the most proficient methods of running businesses. The primary goal and objective of SCM is to increase competitive advantage, add value, and reduce cost globally. Specialization, competency, and the concept of the global supply chain emerged in corporate America in the 1980s to 1990s. This period witnessed in its wake the neglect of vertical integration and outsourcing of those functions to partners. The specialization model resulted in manufacturing and distribution networks composed of various individual supply chains specific to suppliers, producers, and consumers that came together to manufacture, design, distribute, market, sell, and service products.

In this book, we learned that information technology sets the pace to maximize profits in an organization. Innovation is the bedrock of transformational knowledge in human history. Innovation management is the decision made to accomplish sustainable enterprises and economic reality that connect industry, society, and the environment. In corporate America, technology plays a predominant role in leading the global marketplace. Firms and individual countries have gained tremendously from competitive advantage. Countries may become technological leaders in developing or advancing a particular technology and marketing their acquired technological advantage via licensing. The pervasive role of technology in business and industry is overwhelming.

Porter's five forces, as depicted in figure 6.2, evaluate the competitive intensity of the organization's industry by analyzing the market in five dimensions. Competition in the marketplace defines an organizational strategy. Thus, organizational structure is the driving force behind operations and the foundation upon which both short-term and long-term decisions come to fruition. Strategic business management is the key function in management that coordinates the efforts of people to accomplish goals and objectives by using available resources to minimize cost and increase output, productivity, and profitability. Business management also involves organizational leaders setting different goals for the accomplishment of various purposes within an organization.

Summary

In corporate America, a business organization may be large or small. The type, structure, and nature of the business determine its size. Whether organizations are small, medium, or large businesses, each requires strategies to sustain its operations. The word *strategy* is equally significant to an organizational leader as it is to the general of a strong army. Organizational leaders are in short supply of strategies to sustain their business organizations.

Another gratifying outcome from the research of this little book in your hands is the discovery of the concepts of market orientation (MO) and entrepreneurial attitude orientation (EAO). These two principal business concepts are critical in transforming organizational performance of major corporate establishments. MO focuses on providing products and services that respond to both the needs and wants of the targeted consumers. Whereas MO addresses the need to satisfy targeted customers, EAO is the inclination of organizational leaders to respond in a favorable or disapproving manner on the object of their approach. Thus, EAO is an organizational concept that transforms the organizational performance of indigenous entrepreneurs.

Branding is a marketing concept used for establishing customer loyalty to a product or service in a competitive market. Similarly, cost and product differentiation are other powerful tools used by organizations to gain competitive advantage in the marketplace. Toyota of America must differentiate its electric cars from Ford America's products to gain competitive advantage. Likewise, Caterpillar Company must differentiate the cost of its product in order to compete in its global markets. Large companies use product and cost differentials to establish market dominance. In fact, innovation management determines the leader and the follower in an industry. According to extant literature, the majority of today's world millionaires and billionaires are business owners. Succinctly, it is not an exaggeration to sum up the theme of this book in these few bullets:

- The private and public sectors are two intertwining and indispensable building blocks of corporate America.
- Any business that stops innovating will cease being relevant in both the local and global marketplace.
- The global supply chain will continue to transform the exchange of goods and services.
- An information system is a knowledge management system essential to any business success.
- The word *strategy* is equally significant to the General of a strong Army as it is to a business executive. Strategic business management serves as a witty propellant to a successful business.

Appendix

Summary of States Corporation Registration Requirements

STATES	CONTACTS	# OF INCORPORATORS
Alabama	Corporations Division Office of the Secretary of State (334) 242-5324 http://www.sos.state.al.us/ business/corporations.cfm	One person
Alaska	The Division of Banking, Securities and Commerce Department of Community and Economics (907) 465-2521 http://www.dced.state. ak.us/bsc/copdoc.htn	One natural person, at least 18 years old
Arizona	Arizona Corporation Commission Corporate Division (602) 542-3026 http://www.cc.state.az.us/	One person
Arkansas	Secretary of State (501) 682-1010 http://www.sosweb.state.ar.us/	One person
California	Business Program Division (916) 653-2318 http://www.ss.ca.gov/business/ corp/corporate.htm	One or more natural person/ entity

Colorado	Department of State Business Services (303) 894-2251 http://www.sos.state.co.us/ pubs/business/main.htm	One natural person, at least 18 years old
Connecticut	Secretary of the State's Office (806) 509-6001 http://www.sots.state.ct.us/	One or more natural person/ entity
Delaware	State of Delaware Division of Corporations (302) 739-3073 http://www.state.de.us/ corp/index.htm	One or more natural person/ entity
Florida	Division of Corporations (850) 488-9000 http://www.dos.state. fl.us/doc/index.html	One or more natural person/ entity
Georgia	Corporations Division (404) 656-2817 http://www.sos.state. ga.us/corporations/	One or more natural person/ entity
Hawaii	Department of Commerce and Consumer Affairs (808) 586-2744 http://www.businessregistrations. com/index.html	One or more natural person
Idaho	Office of the Secretary of State (208) 334-2300 http://www.idsos.state.id.us	One or more natural person/ entity
Illinois	Secretary of State—Department of Business Services (217) 782-6961 http://www.sos.state.il.us	One or more natural person/ entity—foreign/ domestic
Indiana	Indiana Secretary of State— Business Services (317) 232-6576 http://ai.org/sos/bus_service/	One or more natural person/ entity
Iowa	Business Service Division Office of the Secretary of State (515)281-5204 http://www.sos.state.ia.us/ business/services.html	One or more natural person/ entity

Kansas	Kansas Secretary of State— Corporations Division (785) 296-4564 http://www.kssos.org/ corpwelc.html	One or more natural person/ entity
Kentucky	Kentucky Secretary of State (502) 564-3490 http://www.sos.state.ky.us	One or more natural person/ entity
Louisiana	Louisiana Secretary of State— Commercial Division (225)925-4704 http://www.sec.state.la.us/ comm/comm-index.htm	One or more natural person/ entity
Maine	Maine Department of the Secretary of State Bureau of Corporations, Elections and Commissions (207) 287-4190 http://www.state.me.us/ sos/cec/corp/corp.htm	One or more natural person/ entity
Maryland	Corporate Records (410) 767-1340 http://www.dat.state.md.us/ sdatweb/charter.html	Any one natural person
Massachusetts	The Corporations Division of the Secretary of the Commonwealth's Office (617) 727-9640 http://www.state.ma.us/ sec/cor/coridx.htm	One or more natural person/ entity
Michigan	Bureau of Commercial Services Corporations Division (517) 241-6470 http://www.cis.state.mi.us/corp/	One or more natural person/ entity
Minnesota	Business Services Director Minnesota Secretary of State (651) 296-2803 http://www.sos.state.mn.us/ business/index.html	Any one natural person

Mississippi	Business Services Director Mississippi Secretary of State (601) 359-1633 http://www.sos.state.ms.us/ busserv/corp/corporations.html	One or more natural person/ entity
Missouri	Corporations Division James C. Kirkpartrick State Information Center (573) 751-4153 http://www.mosl.sos.state. mo.us/bus-er/soscor.html	Any one natural person
Montana	Business Services Bureau Secretary of State (406) 444-3665 http://www.state.mt.us/ sos/index.htm	One or more natural person/ entity
Nebraska	Nebraska Secretary of State, Corporate Division (402) 471-4079 http://www.nol.org/business.html	One or more natural person/ entity
Nevada	Corporate Recordings/ Corporate Information Secretary of State—Annex Office (775) 684-5708 http://www.sos.state.nv.us/	Any one natural person
New Hampshire	New Hampshire Secretary of State Corporate Division (603) 271-3244 http://www.webster.state. nh.us/sos/corporate/	One or more natural person/ entity
New Jersey	Division of Revenue (609) 292-9292 http://www.state.nj.us/tresury/ revenue/dcr/dcrpg.1html	One or more natural person/ entity
New Mexico	State Corporation Commission Corporation Department (505) 827-4511	One or more natural person/ entity

New York	New York State Department of State Division of Corporations, State Records and Uniform Commercial Code (518) 474-1418 http://www.dos.state.ny.us/ corp/corpwww.html	One or more natural person/ entity
North Carolina	Corporations Division (919) 807-2225 http://www.secretary.state. nc.us/corporations/	One or more natural person/ entity
North Dakota	Secretary of State (701) 328-4284 E-mail: sosbir@state.nd.us	One or more natural person/ entity
Ohio	Secretary of State Business Services Division (614) 466-3910 http://www.state.oh.us/sos/	One or more natural person/ entity
Oklahoma	Business Records Department (900) 555-2424 http://www.sos.state.ok.us/	Any one natural person
Oregon	Janet Sullivan, Director Corporations Division (503) 986-2200 http://www.sos.state.or.us/ corporation/bic/bic.htm	One or more natural person/ entity
Pennsylvania	Department of State Corporation Bureau (717) 787-1057 http://www.dos.state. pa.us/corp/index.htm	One or more natural person/ entity
Rhode Island	First Stop Business Center (401) 222-2185 http://sec.state.ri.us/ bus/firststp.htm	One or more natural person/ entity
South Carolina	South Carolina Secretary of State (803) 734-2158 http://www.scsos.com/	One or more natural person/ entity

South Dakota	Secretary of State Capitol Building (605) 773-4845 http://www.state.sd.us/sos/sos.htm	Any natural person at least 18 years old
Tennessee	Division of Business Services (615) 741-6488 http://www.state.tn.us/ sos/service.htm	Any natural person at least 18 years old
Texas	Corporations Section Secretary of State (512) 463-5583 http://www.sos.state.tx.us/ corp/index.shtml	Any natural person At least 18 years old
Utah	Utah Department of Commerce Division of Corporations and Commercial Code (801) 530-4849 http://www.commerce.stateut. us/corporat/corpcoc.htm	One or more natural person/ entity
Vermont	Vermont Secretary of State Corporations Division (802) 828-2386 http://www.sec.state.vt.us/ corps/corpindex.htm	Any natural person at least 18 years old
Virginia	Office of the Clerk Virginia State Corporations Division (804) 371-9733 http://www.state.va.us/scc/ division/clk/index.htm	One or more natural person/ entity
Washington	Corporate Division (360) 753-7115 http://www.secstate.wa.gov/ corps/default.htm	One or more natural person/ entity
West Virginia	Corporations Division Secretary of State (304)558-8000 http://www.state.wv.us/ sos/corp/default.htm	One or more natural person/ entity
Wisconsin	Corporations Section, 3rd Floor (608) 267-6813 http://www.wdfi.org/corporations/	One or more natural person/ entity

Wyoming	Secretary of State Corporation Division (307) 777-7311 http://www.soswy.state.wy.us/ corprat/corporat.htm	One or more natural person/ entity

Source: *Own Your Own Corporation - Sutton, G. (2001)*

Glossary

Adinfinitum. Adinfinitum is a Latin word meaning forever, infinity.

Agility. Agility is the power of moving quickly and easily; nimbleness; exercises demanding agility.

Architectural innovation. Architectural innovation is the reconfiguration of an existing product or service technology leaving the components and the core design concepts unchanged.

Bargaining power of suppliers. An analysis of provider characteristics that affect the ability of the organization to negotiate for favorable treatment when purchasing materials or service features of interest.

Blog. A blog is similar to a journal on a website.

Brand equity. Brand equity is one of the marketing strategies a business can develop over time by maintaining a brand's strong name. Brand equity relates to the goodwill or intangible asset of the business.

Branding. Branding is an idea or image of a particular product or service that captures consumers' interest.

Brand loyalty. Brand loyalty is the extent to which a consumer desired and favors buying a particular brand of a product or a service.

Brand strategy. Brand strategy is one of the long-term market planning techniques used to install the company's products or services in the minds of consumers.

Business. A business is a trade or an activity one engages in for profit.

Business intelligence. Business intelligence (BI) is the collective information about organization customers, competitors, partners, environment, and internal operations that enable the organization to make efficient and strategic business decisions.

Business management. Business management is the function in management that coordinates the efforts of people to accomplish goals and objectives by using available resources to minimize cost and increase output, productivity, and profitability.

Capital. The initial amount of money to start up a business.

Company. A company is an artificial person with rights and liabilities.

Competitive advantage. Competitive advantage relates to customizing a product to meet the needs of a specialized market segment.

Competitive strategy. An organization's competitive strategy defines the way in which it positions itself to compete in the marketplace.

Control activity. Control activity is the second level in the hierarchy of management strata.

Control environment. The control environment is the tone at the top, as it is sometimes called.

Corporate. Corporate, as its name implies, means a company or group.

Corporate America. Corporate America refers to the conglomeration of all the elements that make up or constitute the processes involved in the decisions of what goods to produce and how and when to produce them, and all the efforts involved in the distribution of these goods and services to the last consumer within the confines of the American society and the global marketplace.

Corporate social responsibility. As the term implies, corporate social responsibility is a term used in business to refer to the attitude of an organization's response in dealing with its economic, social, and environmental impacts.

Cost leadership. Cost leadership focuses on the organization's ability to sell a high volume of low-cost products.

Cost leadership strategy. Under this approach, an entity will seek to be the low-cost provider in an industry in any given level of output.

Cream of the crop. The best of the bunch.

Creditor. A creditor is someone who has a stake in debt owed.

Database. As the term suggests, a database is a collection of information used to access and organize that information in a logical structure.

Database management systems. As the name suggests, data base management systems (DBMS) assist management to explain the logical organization for a database and access and use the data within that database.

Data dictionary. As the name suggests, a data dictionary contains the logical structure for information in a database.

Data mining. As the name suggests, data mining is the process of designing or configuring an organization's anomalies and the correlations within multiple data sets to predict outcomes.

Data warehousing. Data warehousing (DW) is a logical combination of information garnered from many operational databases and used in decision-making.

Debt. A debt is an amount owed in a business transaction.

Doppelganger brand. A doppelganger brand (carbon copy) is a marketing technique of brand image used to undermine the perceived authenticity of an emotional branding story and, thus, the identity value that the brand provides to consumers.

E-commerce. As the name suggests, e-commerce (electronic commerce) is the organized effort of individuals, businesses, and governments to produce and sell for profit the goods and services that satisfy the needs of society through facilities available on the Internet.

Emotional brand. An emotional brand is one of the marketing strategies to target the emotion of a particular consumer.

Enterprise resource management. Enterprise resource management (ERM) is software that enables an organization to manage user access to its network resources efficiently.

Entity. An entity is a body, unit, or individual.

General partner. A general partner is the partner responsible for the management of a partnership. The general partner also is responsible for the debts of the partnership since the law does not shield the general partner to limited liability in a partnership.

Generic strategies. The two basic generic strategies identified by Porter that provide competitive advantage are (1) cost leadership and (2) differentiation strategies.

Incremental innovation. Incremental innovation is a type of innovation that is used to exploit already existing technologies by changing their forms.

Information technology. As the name implies, information technology (IT) relates to the application of computers and telecommunications equipment to store, retrieve, transmit, and manipulate data, often in the context of business.

Innovation. As the name suggests, innovation relates to creativity or new ideas to alter or create change to existing products or processes.

Innovation management. As the name suggests, innovation management relates to managing innovation processes.

Internal Revenue Code (IRC). The IRC is the federal statutory tax law in the United States of America.

Joint venture. A joint venture (JV) is a business in which the owners accept to develop, for a given time, a new entity, and new assets by contributing capital.

Just in time (JIT). JIT is one of the inventory management strategies used mostly by manufacturing firms to manage inventory.

Knowledge management. Knowledge management is the name of the concepts in which an organization consciously and comprehensively gathers, organizes, shares, and analyzes its knowledge regarding resources, documents, and people's skills.

Liability. A liability is a legal obligation or responsibility a debtor owes to a creditor.

Limited liability. As the term implies, limited liability refers to a limit of the assumption of debts.

Limited liability limited partnership. A limited liability limited partnership (LLLP) is a type of business organization that allows the general partner(s) of a limited partnership to enjoy limited liability, just like limited partners.

Limited partnership. A limited partnership is a type of partnership that allows its partners to exercise limited liability. This type of partnership allows a general partner to manage the business operation on a daily basis and bear the debts of the partnership.

Glossary

Management information systems. Management information systems (MIS) help to facilitate the management process by creating various types of special reports easily.

Monitoring. Monitoring is one of the control elements to ensure that the daily activities of the organization regarding set goals, policies, and procedures are implemented in accordance to set standards.

Obsolescence. The act of not being technologically useful due to wear and tear.

Online analytical processing. Online analytical processing (OLAP) is the use of information to support decision-making within an organization. In most businesses, OLAP is inevitable.

Online transaction processing. Online transaction processing (OLTP) is the garnering of input information, processing that information, and updating existing information to reflect the gathered and processed information.

Organizational learning. As the term implies, organizational learning is the process of producing, sustaining, and circulating knowledge within an organization.

Outsourcing. Outsourcing is a business technique or practice that allows a business to move any of its elements of production to another supply chain to reduce the cost of production or gain competitive advantage.

Partner. A partner is a co-owner or participant in the ownership of a business.

Partnership. A partnership is the association of two or more parties to engage in a business to make profit.

Product differentiation. Product differentiation is a competition technique used by an organization to offer unique features or benefits to the customer (e.g., gasoline that contains additives to improve engine longevity).

Product innovation. Product innovation is a new technology or combination of technologies introduced to meet user needs.

Product leadership. Product leadership is a process of maintaining a competitive advantage by dominating particular markets by providing the best products or services to those markets.

Radical innovation. Radical innovation, as the name implies, is the embodiment, combination, or synthesis of knowledge in original, relevant, and valued new products, processes, or services.

Relational database. A relational database uses a series of logically related two-dimensional tables to store information in the form of a database.

Research and development. Research and development (R&D) are the effort to generate new information or ideas to assimilate and exploit existing information or ideas.

Risk assessment. Risk assessment is one of the five significant elements of internal controls within an organization used to assess inherent business risks.

Sarbanes-Oxley Act of 2002 (SOX). The Sarbanes-Oxley Act of 2002 is mandatory. The US Congress passed this act in 2002 to protect investors from the possibility of fraudulent accounting activities by corporations. SOX mandated strict reforms to improve financial disclosures from corporations and prevent accounting fraud. The enactment of the law was in response to the accounting scandals in the early 2000s. Scandals such as Enron, Tyco, and WorldCom shook investor confidence in financial statements and required an overhaul of regulatory standards.

S corporation. An S corporation is a business organization owned by two or more people in a business arrangement not to exceed one hundred employees.

Search engines. As the name implies, a search engine is a tool on the web to assist the user to find a site for information or service.

Service innovation. Service innovation is taking extra steps to create new ideas on how to improve customer service image as well as treat a customer like a king.

Service leadership. Service leadership, as the term implies, is the power of providing services by leading others to succeed.

Social networking sites. As the name implies, a social networking site is a specific site used to post personal information about oneself, create a network of friends, and share contents such as photographs and the like. It must remain personal, not formal. Such sites popular today include MySpace, with more than 200 million users, and Facebook.

Sole proprietorship. A sole proprietorship is a one-person business.

Strategic management. As the name implies, strategic management is the long-term planning to achieve a set goal or objective.

Strategy. The word *strategy* is a Greek word originated by the military that means long-term planning to accomplish a set objective or goal.

Supply chain. As the name implies, the supply chain is the business concept used to form alliance or partnership relationships laterally or horizontally between one (suppliers) business and another (buyer) to profit.

Supply chain management. Supply chain management (SCM) is a process of managing the supply chain globally or nationally in order to gain competitive advantage.

Sustainable innovation management. Sustainable innovation management relates to a long-term management strategy intended to sustain an organization.

SWOT analysis matrix. The SWOT analysis matrix is a structured planning method used to evaluate the strengths, weaknesses, opportunities, and threats in a particular project or business venture.

Threat of new entrants. As the name suggests, the threat of new entrants refers to the factors that affect the ability of new companies to enter the market.

Threat of substitute products. The threat of substitute products is because the availability of alternative products or technologies limits the competitive strategies available to an organization.

Threats. Threats are environmental elements that can impact the company judgment or projects.

Tort. A tort is an offense or a wrongdoing of an individual to cause harm.

URL. As the name suggests, the uniform resource locator is a unique web page within a specific website.

Web browser. Web browser software enables one to surf the Internet; some examples are Internet Explorer, Firefox, and Google Chrome.

Website. A website is a particular site on the web you can visit.

Website address. A website address is a particular name that signifies and identifies a unique site on the web, for example, www. baseball.com.

References

Abernathy, W. J., & Utterback, J. M. (1978). Patterns of industrial innovation. *Technology Review, 80*(7), 41–47. Retrieved from http://www.technologyreview.com

Al-Debei, M. M., & Avision, D. (2010). Developing a unified framework of the business model concept. *European Journal of Information Systems, 19*(3), 359–376. Retrieved from http://www.palgrave.journal.com/ejis/

Al-Debei, M. M., El-Haddadeh, R., & Avison, D. (2008). Defining the business model in the new world of digital business. *Proceedings of the Americas Conference on Information Systems (AMCIS)*, 1–11. Retrieved from http://www.bura.brunel.ac.uk/bitstream/2438/2887/1/AMCIS2008.pdf

Apple Inc. FY2014 Form 10-K p. 24. Retrieved from http://investor.apple.com/secfiling.cfm? filingid=1193125-14-383437&cik=#D783162D10K_HTM, accessed August 1, 2015.

Aremu, M. A., & Adeyemi, S. L. (2011). Small and medium scale enterprises as a survival strategy for employment generation in Nigeria. *Journal of Sustainable Development, 4*(1), 200–206. doi:10.5539/jsd.v4n1p200

Ashurst, C., Cragg, P., & Herring, P. (2011). The role of IT competencies in gaining value from e-business: An SME case study. *International Small Business Journal, 30*, 640–658. doi:10.1177/0266242610375703

References

Balmer, J. M. (2001). Corporate identity, corporate branding, and corporate marketing—seeing through the fog. *European Journal of Marketing, 35*(3/4), 248–291. doi:10.1108/03090560110694763

Barney, J. B. (2002). *Gaining and sustaining competitive advantage* (2nd ed.). Reading, MA: Addison-Wesley. Retrieved from http://www.anderson.ucla.edu

Berkshire Hathaway Inc. *FY2014 Annual Report*, p. 46. Retrieved from http://www.berkshirehathaway.com//2014ar/2014ar, accessed April 20, 2015.

Beswick, P. (2013, May). *Annual SEC and Financial Reporting*. Remarks presented at the 32nd Institute conference on U.S. Securities and Exchange Commission, Pasadena, CA. Retrieved from http://www.sec.gov/

Blanco, S. (2016). *Toyota Prius prime plugs in with 22 EV miles*. Toyota Corporation. Retrieved from http://www.autoblog.com

Bonanno, G., & Haworth, B. (1998). The intensity of competition and the choice between product and process innovation. *International Journal of Industrial Organization, 16*, 495–510. doi:10.1016/S0167-7187(97)00003-9

Brown, J. (2015). 25 inspirational quotes by the highest performing CEO. *Addicted to Success*. Retrieved from http://www.addicted2success.com

Brown, J. S., & Duguid, P. (1991). Organizational learning and communities-of-practice: Toward a unified view of working, learning, and innovation. *Organization Science, 2*(1), 40–56. doi:10.1287/orsc.2.1.40

Carillon Tower. Retrieved from http://www.necoyote.com/places/charllote.html

Caramela, S. (2016, June). What is corporate social responsibility: Small business solutions & Inspiration. *Business News Daily*,

1-8. Retrieved from http://www.businessnewsdaily.com/4679-corporate social-responsibility.html

Chesbrough, H. W. (2003). *Open innovation: The new imperative for creating and profiting from technology.* Boston, MA: Harvard Business School Press.

Chevron *FY2014 Annual Report,* p. 3. Retrieved from http://www.chevron.com/annualreport/2014, accessed May 30, 2015.

Chevron *FY 2014 Annual Report,* p. 35. Retrieved from http://www.chevron.com, accessed June 30, 2015.

Christensen, C. M. (2011). *The innovator's dilemma.* Harvard Business Review, New York, NY: Harper Collins Publishers.

Christensen, C. M., & Raynor, M. E. (2003). Creating and sustaining successful growth: The innovator's solution. *Soundview Executive Book Summaries, 25,* 2–8. Retrieved from http://www.summar.com

Cohen, W. M., & Levinthal, D. A. (1989). Innovation and learning: The two forces of R & D. *The Economic Journal, 99*(397), 569–596. Retrieved from http:www.jstor.org

Collis, D. J. (2005). *Strategy: Create and implement the best strategy for your business.* Boston: Harvard Business Review Press.

Courtney, T. B. (2002). *The law of private companies* (2nd ed.). Oxford, NY: Bloomsbury Professional. Retrieved from http://www.en.wikipedia.org/

Daintith, J. (2009). *IT: A dictionary of physics* (6th ed.). Oxford, NY: Oxford University Press.

Davenport, H. (2006). *Competing on analysis.* Boston, MA: Harvard Business Review. Retrieved from http://www.hbr.org

Dharan, B. G., & Bufkins, W. R. (2004). *Enron: Corporate Fiascos and their implications*. Foundation Press. Retrieved from http://www.ruf.rice.edu/~bala/files/dharam-bufkins_enron_red_flags.pdf

Estrin, J. (2009). *Closing the innovation gap: Reigniting the spark of creativity in a global economy*. New York: McGraw-Hill.

Exxon Mobil *FY2014 Annual Report*, p. 41. Retrieved from http://www.cdn.exxonmobil.com/~/Media/global/Reports/Summary%20Annual%. Accessed March 15, 2015.

Farahmand, M., & Alinejad, M. (2016). The mobile phone usage and its consequences. *International Journal of Humanities and Cultural Studies*, 536-549. Retrieved from http://www.ijhcs.com/index.php/ijhc/index

FedEx Corporation *FedEx 2015 Annual Report*. Retrieved from http://www.sl.q4cdn. com/714383399/files/doc-financials/annual/FedEx_2015_Annual_Report.pdf. Accessed June 17, 2016.

Florida, R. L., & Kenney, M. (1988). Venture capital-financed innovation and technological change in the USA. *Research Policy, 17*, 119–137. doi:10.1016/0048-7333(88)90038-8

Ford Motors *FY 2014 Annual Report*. Retrieved from http://www.Corporate.ford.com/annual-reports/annual-report-2014/files/201_Ford_Annual_Report _smfromhttp. Accessed April 5, 2015.

Fortune 500 (2012). The Top 10 largest U.S. banks by assets. *Time*, 1-30. Retrieved from http://www.fortune.com/fortune500/

Fortune 500 (2013). The Top 10 largest U.S. corporations by revenue and employment. Time, 1-30. Retrieved from http://www.fortune.com/fortune500/

Fortune 500 (2014). The Top 10 largest U.S. corporations by revenue and employment. *Time*, 1-30. Retrieved from http://www.fortune.com/fortune500/

Gallini, N., & Winter, R. (1985). Licensing in the theory of innovation. *The RAND Journal of Economics, 16*(2), 237–252. Retrieved from http:www.researchgate.net/Publication/24046510

Gallouj, F., & Windrum, P. (2015). Services and services innovation. *Journal of Evolutionary Economics, 19,* 141–148. doi:101007/s00191-008-0123-7

General Electric FY 2014 Annual Report, pp. 3, 4. Retrieved from http://corporate.ge.com/http://corporate.ge.com/annual-reports/annual-report-2014/files/201_General   Electric _Annual_Report_sm.pdf. Accessed August 10, 2015.

General Motors *FY 2014 Annual Report*, p. 66. Retrieved from http://www.gm.com Content/dam/Gmcom/COMPANY/Investors/ Stockholder_Information/_GM_Annual_Report. Accessed August 10, 2015.

George, G., & Bock, A. J. (2012). *Model of opportunity: How entrepreneurs design firms to achieve the unexpected.* New York: Cambridge University Press.

Giannakis, M., & Louis, M. (2011). A multi-agent based framework for supply chain risk management. *Journal of Purchasing & Supply Management, 17,* 23–31. doi: 10.1016/j.pursup.2010.05.001

Godin, B. (2006). The linear model of innovation: The historical construction of an analytical framework. *Science, Technology, & Human Values, 31,* 639–667. doi:10.1177/0162243906291864

Gompers, P. A. (2002). *Corporations and the financing of innovation: The corporate venturing experience.* Boston, MA: Harvard Business Review Press.

Greene, J. (2003, April). Wi-Fi means business: The up-from-the-streets movement is catching on in the corporate world. *Business Week:* Retrieved from http://www.businessweek.com/magazine/ extra.htm

References

Haag, S., & Cummings, M. (2008). *Management information systems: For the information, age* (7th ed.). Boston, MA: McGraw-Hill.

Harvard Business Review. (2011). *Inspiring & executing innovation.* Boston: Harvard Business Review Press Harvard Way, Harvard Business School Publishing Corporation.

Henderson, R. M., & Clark, K. M. (1990). Architectural innovation: The reconfiguration of existing product technologies and the failure of established firms. *Administrative Science Quarterly, 35*(1), 9–30. Retrieved from http: www.jstor.org

Hess, A. E. M. (2013, August). The 10 largest employers in America. U.S Today. Retrieved from http://www.247wallst.com/ special -report/2013/08/16/states-profiting-the-sin/

Hume, T. (2012). Beyond Concord: The next generation of supersonic flight. Retrieved from http://www.cnn.com/2012/08/23/tech/ innovation/beyond-concord-supersonic-flight/

Informationstation.org. Private sector vs. public sector. Retrieved from http://www.informationstation.org/kitchen_table_econ/ private-sector-vs-public-sector/. Accessed June 20, 2015.

Jorgensen, F., & Ulhoi, J. P. (2010). Enhancing innovation capacity in SMEs through early network relationships. *Creativity and Innovation Management, 19,* 397–404. Retrieved from http:// www.researchgate.net/

Kanter, R. M. (2012). Enriching the ecosystem. *Harvard Business Review, 90*(3), 140–147. Retrieved from http://www.hbr.org

Katz, R. (2003). *Managing creativity and innovation: Practical strategies to encourage creativity.* Boston, MA: Harvard Business School Publishing Corporation.

Keller, K. L., & Lehmann, D. R. (2006). Brands and branding: Research findings and future priorities. *Marketing Science, 25,* 740–759. doi:101287/mksc.1050.0153

Kempis, T., & Keynes, J. M. (2015). Quotations and famous quotes by J. F. Kennedy—Proverbs. Retrieved from http://www. en.provverbia.net

Kim, W. C., & Mauborgne, R. (2004). *Blue ocean strategy.* Boston, MA: Harvard Business Review. Retrieved from http://www.hbr

Konsti-Laakso, S., Pihkala, T., & Kraus, S. (2012). Facilitating SME innovation capability through business networking. *Creativity and Innovation Management, 21*(1), 93–105. doi:10.1111/j.1467-8691.2011.00623.x

Kroll, L., & Dotan, K. (2016). The world's billionaires. Retrieved from http://www.forbes.com/billionaires/list/9#

Kumar, S. S. (2009). Risk management in supply chains. *Advances in Management, 2*(11), 36–39. Retrieved from http://www. managein.org

La Paz, A. I., Ramaprasad, A., Syn, T., & Vasquez, J. (2015). An ontology of e-commerce—Mapping a relevant corpus of knowledge. *Journal of Theoretical and Applied Electronic Commerce Research, 10*(2), 1–19. doi:10.4067/s0718-18762015000200001

Laszlo, A., & Laszlo, K. (2004). SEA: Strategic evolutionary advantage: World future. *The Journal of Global Education, 60,* 19–114. doi: 10.1080/725289195

Lee, Yang, Mizerski, & Lambert. (2015). *The strategy of global branding and brand equity.* New York: Routledge.

Mak, P. (2015, December 5). Public company solution: Internal control simplified. *Web log post.* Retrieved from http://www. coso2013solution.com

Man, T. W. Y., Lau, T., & Chan, K. F. (2002). The competitiveness of small and medium enterprises: A concretization with focus on entrepreneurial competencies. *Journal of Business Venturing, 17,* 123–142. Retrieved from http:// www.journals.elsevier.com

Martin, R. (2007). Design and business: Why can't we be friends? Journal of Business Strategy, 6(12), 6-12. doi:10.1108/02756660710760890

McWilliams, A., & Siegel, D. (2000, April). Corporate social responsibility and financial performance: Correlation or misspecification? *Strategic Management Journal, 21*(5), 603–609. doi: 10.1002/(SICI)1097-0266(200005)21:5<603: :AID-SMJ101>3.0.CO;2-3

McWilliams, A., & Siegel, D. (2001, April). Corporate social responsibility: A theory of the firm perspective. *Academy of Management Review, 26*, 117–127. doi:10.5465/amr.2001.4011987

Mentzer, J. T., Myers, M. B., & Stank, T. P. (2007). *Handbook of: Global supply chain management.* Thousand Oaks, CA: Sage Publication, Inc.

Millikin, M. (2016). Worldwide sales of Toyota hybrids surpass 9 million units: Prius family accounts for 63%. *Green Car Congress.* Retrieved from http://www.toyota.com/worldwidesales/

Mintzberg, H. (1987). The strategy concept 1: Five p's for strategy. *California Management Review, 30*(1), 11–24. Retrieved from http://www. sabingroup.com/wp-content/uploads/2015/07/

Moghaddan, B. A., & Armat, P. (2015). A study on the effect of innovation and branding on the performance of small and medium enterprises. *Management Science Letters, 5*, 245–250. doi:10.5267/j.msl.2015.1.015

Murray, A. (2014, June). The 10 top largest corporations in the U.S. by revenues. *Time,* Retrieved from http://www.fortune.com/fortune500

Musteen, M., & Datta, D. K. (2010). Learning about foreign markets: A study of Czech SMEs. *Journal of International Entrepreneur, 9*, 91–109. doi:10.1007/s10843-010-0067-5

Nelson, R. R., & Winter, S. G. (1977). In search of a useful theory of innovation. *Research Policy, 6*(1), 36–76. Retrieved from http://www. elsevier.com/

Office of the United States Trade Representative, Executive Office of the President. (2014). Retrieved from http://www.ustr.gov/trade-agreements/free-trade-agreements/transatlantic-trade-and-investment-partnership-t-tip-12

Parikh, V., & Shar, P. (2015). E-commerce recommendation system using association rule mining and clustering. *International Journal of Innovation & Advancement in Computer Science, 4*, 148–155. Retrieved from http://www.academicscience.co

Pettet, B. G. (2005). *Company law.* Upper Saddle River, NJ: Pearson Education. Retrieved from http://www.en.wikipedia.org/

Philips *FY 2014 Annual Report*, p. 4. Retrieved from http://www.2014. annualreport.philips.com/#!/company-financial-statements. Accessed August 1, 2015.

Porter, M. E. (1998). *Competitive advantage: Creating and sustaining superior performance.* New York: The Free Press.

Porter, M. E. (2008). *On competition: Updated and expanded edition.* Boston: Harvard Business Press.

Pride, W. M., Hughes, R. J., & Kapoor, J. R. (2011). *Foundation of Business* (2nd ed.). Mason, OH: Southwestern Cengage Learning.

Qu, W. G., Pinsonneault, A., Tomiuk, D., Wang, S., & Liu, Y. (2015). The impacts of social trust on open and closed B2B e-commerce: A European-based study. *Information and Management, 52*(2), 151–159. doi:10.1016/j.im.2014.07.002

Ricci, T. (2012, November). Unmanned aerial vehicles soar high. New York, NY: *The American Society of Mechanical Engineers'*, Retrieved from http://www.asme.org/engineering-topics/articles/robotics/unmanned-aerial-vehicles-soar-high

Rockman, H. B. (2004). *Intellectual property law for engineers and scientists*. Piscataway, NJ: John Wiley & Sons,

Ross, S. A., Westerfield, R. W., & Jaffe, J. (2010). *Corporate Finance*. New York: McGraw-Hill, Irwin.

Rowley, J., Baregheh, A., & Sambrook, S. (2011). Towards an innovation-type mapping tool. *Management Decision, 40*(1), 73–86. doi:10.1108/00251741111094446

Semler, R. (2000). *How we went digital without a strategy*. Boston, MA: *Harvard Business Review*. Retrieved from http://www.hbr.org

Senge, P., Smith, B., Kruschwitz, N., Laur, J., & Schley, S. (2010*). The necessary revolution: Working together to create a sustainable world*. New York: Broadway Books.

Shah, J. (2009). Supply chain risk management: Academic perspective. *Management Review, 21*(2), 149–157. Retrieved from http://www.iimb.ernet.in/

Siegel, D., Ly, M., Fraser, G., Miller, S., Silver, C., Kohn, J., et al. (2016, June). *Corporate ladder: Definition and breaking down*. Investopedia. Retrieved from http://www.investopedia.com/terms/c/corporate-ladder.asp

Sobihah, M., Mohamad, M., Ali, N. A. M., & Ismail, W. Z. W. (2015). E-Commerce service quality on customer satisfaction, belief and loyalty: A proposal. *Mediterranean Journal of Social Sciences, 6*(2), 260–266. doi:10.5901/mjss.2015.v6n2p260

Srinivasan, S. S., Anderson, R., & Ponnavolu, K. (2002). Customer loyalty in e-commerce: An exploration of its antecedents and consequences. *Journal of Retailing, 78*(1), 41–50. doi:10.1016/S0022-4359(01)00065-3

Stacey, R. D. (2011). *Strategic management and organizational dynamics: The challenge of complexity* (6th ed.). Harlow, England: Pearson, Prentice Hall.

Subramanian, M., & Youndt, M. A. (2005). The influence of intellectual capital on the types of innovative capabilities. *Academy of Management Journal, 46,* 450–463. doi:10.5465/AMJ.200517407911

Sutton, G. (2001). *Own your own corporation: Why the rich own their companies and everyone else works for them.* New York, NY: Warner Books, Inc.

Tang, O., & Nurmaya, M. S. (2011). Identifying risk issues and research advancements in supply chain risk management. *International Journal of Production Economics, 133*(1), 25–34. doi: 10.1016/j.ijpe.2010.06.013

Taylor, T. (2013). 50 greatest presidential quotes of all time. Retrieved from http://www.brainyquote.com/

Tennant, M. (2014, June). Private sector vs public sector. *The New American Magazine.* 1-3. Retrieved from http://www.information station.org/kitchen_table_econ/private sector-vs-public- sector/

Thompson, C. J., Rindfleisch, A., & Arsel, Z. (2006). Emotional branding and the strategic value of the doppelganger brand image. *Journal of Marketing, 70,* 50–64. doi:10.1509/jmkg.2006.70.1.50

Tödtling, F., Lehner, P., & Kaufmann, A. (2009). Do different types of innovation rely on specific kinds of knowledge interactions? *Technovation, 29,* 59–71. doi:10.1016/j.technovation.2006.05.002

Toyota, A. (2016). Worldwide sales of Toyota Hybrid surpass 9 million units. Toyota, Retrieved from http://www.toyota.com/worldwidesales/

Tuncel, G., & Alpan, G. (2010). Risk assessment and management for supply chain networks: A case study. *Computers in Industry, 61,* 250–259. doi: 10.1016/j.compind.2009.09.008

Undercoffler, D. (2016, August). Toyota looks to boost Prius with all-new plug-n Prime. *Automotive News*. Retrieved from http://www.automoyivenews.com

United States Department of Labor. (2012). *News brief: Women retirement security*. Washington DC. Retrieved from http://www.dol.gov

United States Postal Service. (2015). *Retirement funding and payment defaults*. Retrieved from http://www.usps.gov

Utterback, J. M., & Abernathy, W. J. (1975). A dynamic model of process and product innovation. *Omega, The International Journal of Management Science, 3*, 639–655. doi:10.1016/0305-0483(75)90068-7

Valero *FY 2014 Annual Report*, p. 3. Retrieved from http://www.valero.com/Financialpercentage20Documents, Valero_Annual_Report_2014,Web.pdf. Accessed May 30, 2015.

Wal-Mart Stores, Inc *FY 2014 Annual Report*, pp. 18–38. Retrieved from http:www.walmart.com Report/2014_Summary_Annual Report. Accessed July 31, 2015.

Winarsky, N. (2015, September). *How we did it: The president of SRI Ventures on bringing siri to life*. Boston, MA: *Harvard Business Review*. Retrieved from http://www.hbr.org

Wikimedia Foundation, (2015, August). List of largest corporations by revenue. *Wikipedia*. Retrieved from http://www.wikipedia.org/list_of_largest_companies_by_revenue

Wood, D. (1991). Corporate social performance revisited. Retrieved from http://www.jstor.org/stable/258977

Xanthopoulos, A., Vlachos, D., & Lakovou, E. (2011). Optimal newsvendor policies for dual-sourcing supply chains: A disruption risk management framework. *Computers & Operations Research, 39*(2), 350–357. doi: 10.1016/j.cor.2011.04.010

Yang, B., & Yang, Y. (2010). Postponement in supply chain risk management: A complexity perspective. *International Journal of Production Research, 48*, 1901–1912. doi:10.1080/00207540902791850

Zhu, W. (2005). Robust supply chain design mechanisms: Applications to risk management, coordination, and multiple-modular design (Doctoral dissertation). Available from ProQuest Dissertations and Theses database (UMI No. 3192833).

Index